The New Reformation?

Senior Novitiate Library

BOOKS BY JOHN A. T. ROBINSON
Published by The Westminster Press

The New Reformation?
Christian Morals Today
Liturgy Coming to Life
Honest to God
On Being the Church
   in the World

THE
New Reformation?

by

JOHN A. T. ROBINSON
BISHOP OF WOOLWICH

Senior Novitiate Library

6-0083

THE WESTMINSTER PRESS
PHILADELPHIA

© SCM PRESS LTD 1965

LIBRARY OF CONGRESS CATALOG CARD NO. 65-17645

Published by The Westminster Press ®
Philadelphia, Pennsylvania

PRINTED IN THE UNITED STATES OF AMERICA

CONTENTS

	Preface	7
1	Troubling of the Waters	9
2	Starting from the Other End	32
3	Towards a Genuinely Lay Theology	54
4	Living in the Overlap	78
	Postscript	101
	Appendix I Can a Truly Contemporary Person *not* be an Atheist?	106
	II Spiritual Education in a World without Religion *by Ruth Robinson*	123
	Index	141

PREFACE

THIS book is an expanded and revised version of material given in May 1964 as the Purdy Lectures at Hartford Seminary, Connecticut, and as the Thorp Lectures at Cornell University. I am most grateful for the hospitality, the stimulus and the encouragement of all my friends in the United States. I have altered the material so that it is now addressed in the first instance to the only church situation I can claim to know from the inside. But I have deliberately borne in mind a transatlantic audience, and for this reason made frequent reference to the exciting amount of new thinking that is going on on both sides of the water, in the hope that this will assist the process of cross-fertilization.

Since this book was in proof there have been two further contributions from across the Atlantic. The first was he long article in *Time* for 25 December 1964 on 'Christian Renewal'. In a notable piece of journalism it showed how remarkably widespread is the sense of an 'eve of Reformation' spirit running through the Church, demanding of it an openness to quite radical change in its new secular setting. Then in January 1965 McClelland and Stewart of Toronto published what I think to be the most penetrating and, indeed, prophetic book by an outsider taking a critical look at the Church, *The Comfortable Pew*, by the leading Canadian writer and journalist, Pierre Berton. The fact that it was officially commissioned by the Anglican Church in Canada (despite explosive protests) is itself a sign of real hope.

I have included, as appendices, a lecture given at the opening of an Exhibition on Atheism, Eastern and Western, at the University of Frankfurt in November 1964, and one by my wife at the Episcopal Theological School, Cambridge, Massachusetts in May 1964 and subsequently at the Evangelical Academy, East Berlin.

JOHN WOOLWICH

1

TROUBLING OF THE WATERS

A New Reformation—Less or More?

THE seed of these lectures germinated in Rome on 2 January 1964. Before that it had been lying around in the drawers of my mind. But it was activated into growth by a remark made to me by Cardinal Bea, the wonderfully gracious head of the Vatican Secretariat for Christian Unity. 'The Counter-Reformation', he said, 'is over.' By that he meant that the whole period during which the life of the Roman Catholic Church has been conditioned by reaction to Protestantism is now at an end. News of the cessation of hostilities may doubtless take some time to reach certain sections of the front. Nevertheless, the significance of the remark, coming from such a source, cannot easily be exaggerated.

But it made me realize that one could only say that—and rejoice in it—if one went on to the corresponding recognition that 'the Reformation is over'. And this would be received with alarm in many breasts. By that, of course, I do not mean that the consequences of the Reformation divide are now a thing of the past. We shall go on living with them for a long time. Nor do I mean that the issues on which we split are no longer real. In one sense nothing has changed. If challenged on the infallibility of the Pope or the assumption of the Virgin Mary I have not shifted my position, nor have the Romans moved from theirs. In that sense we are no nearer, nor indeed has a single step been taken towards organic unity. And yet in another sense everything has changed. Suddenly we find ourselves in a different atmosphere and fighting a different war. The old entrenchments are still there, lined up against each other, and the rifle bullets continue from time to time to cleave the air. Every now and again, indeed, the fusillade flares up—and it only takes a trivial incident to show that the old suspicions and animosities are far from dead. Nevertheless, the fighting on this front has been cooling off for some time. No one any longer has much zeal for it. It has been overtaken and left behind by a new war of movement, in which to our surprise, and some embarrassment, we find ourselves fighting side by side. We realize as we watch the Vatican Council, and as Roman Catholics watch, and catch up on, many of the movements in the Reformed Churches, that their advances are our advances and *vice versa*. No longer do we feel that ground can be gained on one front only at the expense of the other. The period of civil war in Western Christendom is rapidly drawing to a close, engulfed in a larger campaign in which we can no longer afford to be divided—and no longer want to be.

In that sense the Reformation is over. Let it go. It is the end of an era. But none of this adds up to saying that we are trembling on the verge of a new Reformation. The streams of lava have cooled and hardened from the old eruption. But that in itself does not betoken a new one. A 'New Reformation'? What right have we to talk like this? A convulsion such as shook Europe in the sixteenth century is not something we can expect every year, nor every century. It is not even something we can *want*. It means the dissolution of one world and the birth-pangs of another.

Nevertheless there is just such talk. All of a sudden it seems to be in the air. It is mooted in the journals.[1] It is proclaimed with confidence by an otherwise cautious Canon of Winchester Cathedral, who begins his latest book, *The Ferment in the Church*, with the words: 'The prospect of a New Reformation is clearly in sight. . . . The storm signals are quite unmistakable. . . . No way of halting it exists.'[2] Professor T. F. Torrance of Edinburgh, who regards this ferment as a deplorable

[1] E.g. the whole of *The London Quarterly and Holborn Review* for October 1964 is devoted to a symposium on this theme, with the initiating article by David L. Edwards.

[2] Roger Lloyd, *op. cit.* (SCM Press, London, and Morehouse Barlow, New York, 1964), p. 7.

aberration, nevertheless sees the process as still further advanced: 'Without doubt we are in the midst of a vast new Reformation—it shows a steady and ineluctable advance in spite of wilder and more extravagant theologies and movements which appear on the flanks of the Church's forward march.'[1] A writer in the *Contemporary Review*[2] has even committed the extravagance of comparing *Honest to God*[3] with the nailing of Luther's theses to the church door at Wittenberg.[4]

I am not so sure. All this is a good deal too fast for me. And I certainly see myself in no such role—though I cannot fail to sympathize with Luther's reflections written a year later: 'It is a mystery to me how my theses, more so than my other writings, indeed, those of other professors, were spread to so many places. . . . Had I anticipated their widespread popularity, I would certainly have done my share to make them more understandable.'[5]

Indeed, I believe it is a real question whether a new *Reformation* is the right category at all. From one point of view it is too large a one; from another I suspect it is too small.

It is too large because, in the nature of the case, the present ferment is far more likely to represent what Dr Alec Vidler in his *20th Century Defenders of the Faith*[6] calls (without depreciation) a 'theological fashion' than a turning-point of Church history. Nevertheless it is bound to leave the questions asked subtly different from what they were before. If the comparison

---

[1] 'A New Reformation?', *The London Quarterly and Holborn Review*, October, 1964, p. 293; to be reprinted in *Theology in Reconstruction* (SCM Press, London, and Westminster Press, Philadelphia).

[2] Reginald A. Smith, 'The Organic Way with "Dangerous Thoughts"', November 1963, pp. 223-31.

[3] SCM Press, London, and Westminster Press, Philadelphia, 1963.

[4] There was nothing particularly dramatic in that action: it was 'the usual procedure for giving notices of such disputations, which were a regular feature of University life' (H. Bettenson, *Documents of the Christian Church*, Oxford University Press, 1943, pp. 260-8, where the Theses are reprinted).

[5] 30 May 1518, quoted in *The Reformation in its Own Words*, ed. H. J. Hillerbrand (SCM Press, London, and Harper and Row, New York, 1964), p. 54.

[6] SCM Press, London, 1965.

with 1517 is indeed inflated, the controversies of 1963 may well have their closest parallel in 1860, when the publication of *Essays and Reviews*[1] produced a strikingly similar upheaval, which Dr Vidler himself has vividly described in his other volume, *The Church in an Age of Revolution*.[2] Indeed, I should hope that the effect of such ferment as there has been will be more that of the leaven of liberality introduced by these essayists and men like F. D. Maurice, than of the organized movements set in train by the Evangelical and Tractarian revivals. For in the long run those who change history most are not those who supply a new set of answers but those who allow a new set of questions. And it was indeed this latter possibility, rather than the theological and ecclesiastical systems in which their work took shape, that represented the real achievement of the Reformers.

But while it would be absurd and presumptuous to exaggerate the signs of the times, there is, I think, another sense in which a new Reformation may actually be an inadequate category in which to compass the crisis of our age.

On a world scale, such as we are forced to use today, the old Reformation cannot but look a rather provincial quarrel within the confines of the Christian West. It is certain that any theological revolution that will match our hour cannot be a purely Western product. But I am sure too that the reappraisal cannot be confined to Christendom. Dr Geoffrey Parrinder's book, *The Christian Debate: Light from the East*,[3] is a salutary reminder that Christians can no longer indulge in domestic discussion as though the other world-religions scarcely existed. Certainly my post has brought evidence enough that everything we say is now overheard. I could wish I were better equipped myself to take part in this wider debate.[4] But I welcome, rather than fear, the sympathy with which much that

---

[1] To which, indeed, *Soundings* (ed. A. R. Vidler, Cambridge University Press, 1962) was deliberately seen as a successor a century later.
[2] Penguin Books, London, 1961, ch. XI.
[3] Gollancz, London, 1964.
[4] See Paul Tillich, *Christianity and the Encounter of the World Religions* (Columbia University Press, New York and London, 1963).

I said in *Honest to God* has been received by many within the Hindu and Buddhist traditions. I cannot agree with the (otherwise sympathetic) reviewer in the *Indian Journal of Theology* that 'if this interpretation of Christianity were to prove true, it would mean the end of the mission of Christianity.'[1] Of course, its inadequacies of statement on this flank (on which, like many others, I was not consciously guarding myself!) must be countered by those more competent. But I have not the least desire to weaken or deny the distinctive affirmations of the Christian faith. Among these I should certainly wish to assert: (1) The centrality of the confession 'Jesus is Lord', in the full New Testament sense that 'in him all things cohere'[2] and 'in him the whole fulness of the deity dwells bodily';[3] and (2) the centrality of the utterly *personal* relationship of communion with God summed up in Jesus' address 'Abba, Father!' As long as these affirmations are safeguarded, I am glad if my questioning of the necessity of the 'supranaturalistic' cast of thought (by which the *reality* of God in human experience is represented by the *existence* of gods or of a God in some other realm 'above' or 'beyond' the world in which we live) appears to Hindus, as well as to modern secular men, to make Christian truth less alien to them. For this picture of the universe is certainly not distinctively Christian (it is supremely illustrated in the Olympian religion of ancient Greece), though it may be characteristically Western.

But the adequacy of 'Reformation' as a category for our times is challenged by something still more fundamental than the spiritual geography of the debate. A Reformation presupposes that the Church can be re-formed and a positive answer given to the question, 'Can these bones live?'[4] There is, however, much from within the organized Church, and still more for those observing it from without, to raise the question rather insistently: 'Can it possibly be the carrier of the new life for the new age?' Is the Church not an archaic and well-

[1] J. C. Hindley, January-March 1964, p. 9.
[2] Colossians 1.17.
[3] Colossians 2.9.
[4] Ezekiel 37.3.

protected institution for the preservation of something that is irrelevant and incredible? Because it is so dug in, it will not, of course, disappear overnight, at any rate in Europe and North America—though who can say even that for Afro-Asia? But will it necessarily be the channel of the Spirit? May not the really significant movements of renewal take place outside it and despite it? There are more in our generation than in any previous Christian century who would be inclined to return a reluctant, or not so reluctant, 'Yes' to that question. Thus, so sympathetic a critic—and so typical a twentieth-century man—as Arthur Koestler, yearning as deeply as anyone for restoring 'the divided house of faith and reason', has written: 'Man enters upon a spiritual ice-age; the established churches can no longer provide more than Eskimo huts where their shivering flock huddles together'.[1]

And it is not only from outside that the reformability of the Church, with its theological and institutional inheritance, is seriously questioned. Thus William Hamilton, Professor of Christian Theology and Ethics at Colgate Rochester Divinity School, Rochester, New York, whose seminal book *The New Essence of Christianity*[2] catches the mood of 'the left' in contemporary theology as well as any, writes: 'The God of the Augustinian-Reformed tradition is not only remote, he is irrelevant; he is not only far from us, he has departed from us. It is a very short step, but a critical one, to move from the otherness of God to the absence of God.'[3] And he follows this up more recently in an article, 'Thursday's Child: The Theologian Today and Tomorrow',[4] describing the current alienation, as he sees it, between theology and the Church.

[1] 'The Trail of the Dinosaur', *Encounter*, May 1955.
[2] Association Press, New York, 1961.
[3] *Op. cit.*, p. 55. See Appendix I; also Gabriel Vahanian, *The Death of God* and *Wait Without Idols* (Braziller, New York, 1961 and 1964), and Albert van den Heuvel, 'A World Without God' in *The Death of the Church*, the unpublished report of a British SCM Conference to which I shall be referring again, held at Swanwick 28 December 1963 to 2 January 1964. This and his other lecture, 'The Humiliation of the Church', are to published in a collection of his essays by the SCM Press.
[4] *Theology Today*, January 1964, pp. 487-95.

It used to be otherwise. Before, the theologian would distinguish between God, Christendom, Christianity, and church, so that a different balance of 'yes' and 'no' could be uttered to each. Now he finds himself equally alienated from each of the realities represented by the four terms, and he says his 'no' to each. . . .

The theologian, however, is neither despairing nor hopeful about the church. He is not interested, and he no longer has the energies or interest to answer ecclesiastical questions about 'What the Church Must Do to Revitalize Itself'. . . .

He must live outside. He is not thereby a happier man, nor is he a troubled one. He is neither proud nor guilty. He has just decided that this is how it has to be, and he has decided to say so.

I personally dissent from his conclusion. But, before we talk too glibly about the New Reformation and 'What the Church Must Do to Revitalize Itself', we should weigh such words. We have learnt to live with the idea that modern secular man, whether as an industrial worker or as an intellectual, is deeply estranged from the traditional life and teaching of the churches. So it should not surprise us if this same estrangement asserts itself when he turns theologian. Those of us brought up as 'insiders' are inclined instinctively to feel that if a man is on the way out of the Church we need not take what he says too seriously. But we have to recognize the fact that some of the best younger minds, both among clergy and laity, are nearing this position—and asserting it in the name of Christ. Certainly I know few today who would rally to the call 'On to orthodoxy'.[1] The movement is in the other direction; and there are many who would sympathize with the German theological student quoted by Dr Vidler:[2] 'We must try to be at one and the same time *for* the Church and *against* the Church. They alone can serve her faithfully whose consciences are continually exercised as to whether they ought not, for Christ's sake, to leave her.' As one who knows in his bones that he could not put himself outside, I want to plead for those who feel that they must.

[1] The title of a widely influential book in the previous generation by D. R. Davies (Hodder and Stoughton, London, 1939).
[2] 20*th Century Defenders of the Faith*, p. 122.

At the same time I want to disagree with them, by going on to insist that for me the tension cannot be broken. I cannot renounce the question of what the Church must do to revitalize itself. I believe in fact that re-formation is a category we must use, and my continued exploration of what a new Reformation might mean is testimony to this ineluctable conviction. Until it is finally proved otherwise, the Christian must believe that the Church—and he himself as a member of it—can be used rather than discarded: 'Be it unto me according to thy will.'

But, by the same token, he cannot command renewal. A new Reformation is not something *we* can decide to have. Men may discern the need for it, and the cry may go up for it. Bishop E. R. Wickham, in his prophetic book *Church and People in an Industrial City*[1] closes with precisely such a call: 'What is required is no less than over-all reform.' But, in the words with which Professor Owen Chadwick begins his Pelican on *The Reformation*,[2] 'For a century or more Western Europe had sought for reform of the Church "in head and members" and had failed to find it.' Wycliffe and Huss had come and had gone—before their time. It needed to wait upon the moment, and the movement, of the Spirit.

If today voices are beginning to speak of a new Reformation it is because, perhaps, we can sense that moment and movement again. We cannot be sure: there was many a false dawn before, and I suspect the night must get much darker yet. But the speed of change is so much swifter today that we cannot afford to neglect even the first signs of it—lest we be overtaken by it.

Rustlings and Rumblings

For the Christian, reformation, at any deep level, is not a policy or a programme—though it requires both these. It is a response to a motion of the Spirit. And this perhaps more than anything else distinguishes the Christian from the non-Christian

[1] Lutterworth Press, London, 1957, p. 273.
[2] Penguin Books, London, 1964, p. 11.

humanist. There is an important sense, as I shall be saying, in which the Christian too can, and must, be a humanist. But humanism in its modern sense, as a self-sufficient system, is essentially a do-it-yourself philosophy. Man has to make his own destiny and shape his own values. For the Christian, however, life is essentially a response, a hearkening unto obedience. For the Christian lives by the conviction, the trust, that in and through and under all the relationships of this world there meets him a grace and a demand in whose service alone is to be found life and peace and freedom. And thus the openness is all.

The prerequisite, then, of reformation, as of all else, is sensitivity—sensitivity to what the Spirit is saying to the churches, and to the world. What hour is it? 'Watchman, what of the night?'[1] Is it a 'day of small things'[2]—in which the obedience consists simply of going on going on, tidying up 'here a little, there a little'?[3] Or is it the prelude to great stirrings in which all our structures may be engulfed and reshaped?

Until recently I think I should have said it was the former. But almost overnight one is conscious of the ground moving under one's feet. There *is* a ferment in the Church, which even a couple of years ago I think no one could have predicted. There were indeed many streams of renewal—liturgical, biblical, ecumenical—but they were quiet rivulets gradually filling the old watercourses and silently overflowing their banks. But this was very different from the bubbling up that seems to have been taking place all around us, breaking surface apparently independently in widely different places and yet in such a way that observers have at once discerned a common ferment. There has been a troubling of the waters[4] such as betokens the quickening power of the Spirit, a rustling in the tree-tops such as David was given as a sign that the Lord had passed on before him and that he must act.[5]

All that a Reformation does is to liberate the power that is

---

[1] Isaiah 21.11.   [2] Zechariah 4.10.   [3] Isaiah 28.10.
[4] John 5.1-9.   [5] II Samuel 5.24.

there: it does not generate it. That was Luther's unwitting contribution—to enable what had been building up to burst forth. And what persuades me that a similar break-through may be upon us is the sense of release which has marked the response of recent months. I would fully agree that the first reaction has been primarily negative. As Ralph Morton put it in *The Coracle*,[1] the journal of the Iona Community in Scotland, 'Few people have said: "Now, at last, we understand what the Christian faith really means." Rather they have said: "Now, at last, we know a lot of things that the Christian faith need not mean." ' There is a gasp of relief at being able to express one's questionings and doubts and find them shared. It is significant that two of the books in which people have found greatest liberation should have been called *Objections to Christian Belief*,[2] produced by a theological faculty, and *God is No More*, written by an Anglican parson and his wife.[3]

But it would be a great mistake to read this response as merely confirming unbelief. On the contrary, I believe its power is due to the fact that faith has been let loose. The response of men to Luther's negations was not 'Now we need not believe', but 'Now we *can* believe. If we had had to accept all that as the price of it, we could not. But now we can see that it may be possible.' Men found a similar creative liberation in the words of Jesus. 'What caught men's attention', says Ralph Morton, 'and aroused their opposition were the things he did not believe in and told men not to believe in.' And the same was true of St Paul over circumcision and the Law. But it is the positive that is allowed to shine through the negative which has the power. The Ninety-five Theses nailed on the door at Wittenberg contained no mention of justification by faith: they were an attack on Indulgences. But they allowed the gospel of grace to break through. In the same way Dietrich Bonhoeffer may be best known for the negative phrase

[1] March 1964, p. 2.
[2] Ed. A. R. Vidler, Constable, London, and J. B. Lippincott, Philadelphia, 1963.
[3] Werner and Lotte Pelz, Gollancz, London, and J. B. Lippincott, Philadelphia, 1963.

TROUBLING OF THE WATERS

'religionless Christianity'. But the power he has exercised over our generation has lain in the liberating discovery that secular man *can* be a Christian without having to disown his age. On the face of it, too, Paul van Buren's book *The Secular Meaning of the Gospel*[1] appears, very largely, to reduce and to destroy. The exhilaration it produces in many is due to the fact that when cartloads of metaphysics have been rolled away the Easter light seems all the whiter!

'I am quite sure', wrote the young Luther, 'that the Church will never be reformed unless we get rid of canon law, scholastic theology, philosophy and logic as they are studied today, and put something else in their place.'[2] If pressed about *what* he would put in their place, I suspect he would have been less sure. I have every sympathy with him. In fact, however, what shone through was *not* what he put in their place (his successors filled the gap with an equally deadly Protestant scholasticism) but what he left exposed. If *Honest to God* has spoken to many to whom it was not addressed, it is because they have instinctively recognized through the dust of demolition the God they had lost. Those for whom his image was painted on the old walls see not a ferment but a fog.

But there is, nevertheless, a real difference today. The old Reformation immediately produced its own confessions, its hymns, its models of church order, its denominations. In this sense, it had indeed some very positive things to put in the place of the old. And they sprang fully armed from the head of Jove. It was an age of affirmation, of confident altercation, of theological and national reconstruction. But today the mood is different. It has been well caught in the opening words of the preface to *Soundings*:[3] 'The authors of this volume of essays cannot persuade themselves that the time is ripe for major works of theological construction or reconstruction. It is a time for ploughing, not reaping; or, to use the metaphor we have chosen for our title, it is a time for making soundings, not charts or maps.'

[1] Macmillan, New York, and SCM Press, London, 1963.
[2] Quoted, Owen Chadwick, *op. cit.*, p. 46.   [3] P. ix.

As the Preacher of Ecclesiastes saw,[1] 'There is a time to break down, and a time to build up, ... a time to keep silence and a time to speak.' And the second Reformation, if it comes, will be distinguished from the first by the fact that it is a time of reticence, of stripping down, of travelling light. The Church will go through its baggage and discover how much it can better do without, alike in doctrine and in organization.

I referred earlier to the image of the Church as 'an archaic and well-protected institution for the preservation of something that is irrelevant and incredible'. The twentieth century so far has seen strenuous, and not unsuccessful, efforts to rid the Church of its archaism and irrelevance. In the Church of England, for instance, the primacy of William Temple surely produced evidence that it need not be irrelevant, that of Geoffrey Fisher that it need not be quite so archaic. Under the latter, a formidable list of reforms were put in train to bring it, creakingly, into the twentieth century—new canons and new courts, a new English Bible and a new liturgical commission, a revised psalter and a revised catechism, schemes for redundant churches and schemes for Christian unity, an overhaul of the Church's finances and machinery of government, a major investigation into the payment and deployment of the clergy, etc. These reforms cannot be dismissed, nor, with the possible exception of the new canons (of which I judge the fewer we have the better), must they be allowed to get lost in the sand. The Church of England has undoubtedly changed more quickly over the past twenty years than at any time since the Elizabethan settlement. And yet the more it changes, the more it remains the same! Indeed, the very fact that it is more relevant and cannot so readily be dismissed as archaic means that it appears to be better protected than ever, and what lies under the shell seems just as incredible. And in all this, I should judge, the Church of England has been not untypical.

Moreover, even the movements—biblical, liturgical and ecumenical—which during this period have been revivifying

[1] Ecclesiastes 3.1-8.

the internal life of our churches all share a common limitation. As David Edwards has pointed out:[1]

> *They do not necessarily concern the truth of Christianity.* Theologians and preachers can wax enthusiastic about the 'acts of God' in the Bible without tackling the awkward questions whether God exists and whether, if so, he is credibly revealed to the twentieth century. In a parish of 10,000 the liturgical movement can confine itself to the outward (not the inner) lives of the 200 who will meet as the churchgoers of a particular denomination. The reunion of the churches as they are could be a marriage of the senile, and an 'ecumenical' agreement between Christians on the basis of their common tradition could be purchased at the price of excluding the awkward questions and needs of the irreligious moderns. For some time, therefore, thoughtful Christians have been coming to see that, if the biblical message is to be heard through the churches in our time, a deeper renewal is needed, which may involve a costlier change.

It is this deeper renewal and costlier change which we must mean if we are to talk seriously about a new Reformation—not simply an extension of the present lines of reform (however necessary), which presuppose the continuance of the given structure. I should like, therefore, in the remainder of this chapter to look in a preliminary way at what this could require, both in the field of theology and of organization, if we are really to face the possibility of a new Reformation in our time.

Shaking of the Foundations

First, I would say that the very fact that the basic truth of Christianity is itself at issue, that even God is at hazard, and that nothing is being left unquestioned, is surely a sign that a new thing is upon us. This is not just a continuation of planned reform. Indeed, it is not what was envisaged at all. Of the previous Reformation, Owen Chadwick has written:[2]

---

[1] *The Honest to God Debate*, ed. D. L. Edwards (SCM Press, London, and Westminster Press, Philadelphia, 1963), p. 20.
[2] *Op. cit.*, pp. 13-14.

> When churchmen spoke of reformation, they were almost always thinking of administrative, legal, or moral reformation; hardly ever of doctrinal reformation. . . . They sometimes talked of a theology which should be less remote from human beings, more faithful to the Gospel, a faith which should be less external and more akin to the teaching of the Lord. But to gain this end they had neither desire nor expectation of anything which could be called a change in doctrine.

The parallel today is close.[1] I observed in *Honest to God*[2] that, of the radical thinking I was concerned to bring to the surface, 'I doubt whether any sign of it could be traced in however prolonged a perusal of *The Chronicle of the Convocation of Canterbury*'. All the reforming zeal which I listed before was able to go on, and be recorded, without any reference to the need for a much deeper shaking of the foundations. No one seriously imagined the doctrine of God might be involved, or connected 'putting our house in order' with the distractions of a 'new theology'. At least now, for good or for ill, *The Chronicle of Convocation* bears its imprint, for the greater part of the Archbishop's Presidential Address in May 1963 had to be devoted to it.

But, more seriously, the whole theological front is now wide open: the very foundations are exposed. This I cannot but believe is a healthy and a hopeful thing. In the process there is nothing that will not be questioned, and many things will be shaken. But at least the impression has been shattered, described to me by the agnostic President of the Union at one of our modern Universities, that theology is simply a debate between a closed circle of mandarins within the agreed terms of their system. It has been seen to be a genuinely open-ended search for the truth, and this has raised again the possibility of faith for him as for many others.

But the corollary of this is a readiness on the part of theo-

---

[1] Canon Lloyd has said, 'The trumpet has been blown first in the field of theology. Reformations always do begin here' (*op. cit.*, p. 7). This is factually untrue—particularly of the previous English Reformation. But it may be the point at which a reform movement becomes a reformation—when the root is touched and not merely the branch.

[2] P. 26. .

logians today to come out from behind their prepared positions. As the Editor of *Soundings* puts it again,[1] 'We can best serve the cause of truth and of the Church by candidly confessing where our perplexities lie, and not by making claims which, so far as we can see, theologians are not at present in a position to justify.' Theology will carry conviction not by the assurance of its answers but by the integrity of its questioning, and by the rigour with which it is seen to respect the critical disciplines, historical, scientific and linguistic, of the world it would serve. We must be prepared to be stripped down to the few things we can trust, and not be worried by the many things we do not know. For there is more authority in honest silence than in all the second-hand systems of dogma. 'On the borders', said Bonhoeffer, the John the Baptist of the new Reformation, 'it seems to me better to hold our peace.'[2]

Whereas previously theology was supposed to have an answer for every 'ultimate' question, to supply a spiritual map of the universe on which the edges were as clear as the centre (so that medieval theology could discourse with confidence on limbo and purgatory, and Reformation theology dismiss them with equal confidence), now, I believe, we must recognize that at the borders there is a limited amount that can be said. Like Job, we cannot deny, and yet we cannot speak—in the sense of producing answers for every enquiry in space and time. The great classic doctrines of the creation and governance of the world, predestination and election, pre-existence and immortality, the generation and procession of the Persons of the Trinity, angels and the Devil, heaven and hell, the last judgment and the second coming—these cannot be painted with the assurance or the detail on the wide canvases beloved of our forefathers. For as soon as we pass beyond the limited area verifiable in the experience of our relationships with other people and with things, there is nothing to count for or against

[1] P. ix.
[2] *Letters and Papers from Prison* (SCM Press, London, 1953), p. 124. (In the USA, *Prisoner for God*, Macmillan, New York, 1957.) This theme is powerfully expounded by William Hamilton in the first chapter of *The New Essence of Christianity*, 'On Theological Style'.

the truth of our assertions. What we can say is that the quality, the givenness, the unconditionality, of our relationship to God in Christ would be contradicted if what these doctrines have sought to safeguard were simply denied. We must hold on to them therefore as limiting concepts. But we cannot expatiate on them or make them thrill for our generation with the power they had—and may well have again—for others less critically conditioned.

And all this is no cause for oppression. It can be a source of freedom and liberation. For there is an agnosticism which releases, and allows the Christian to tread with a lighter step. This is the air one breathes in the book of van Buren's I mentioned, which (for all the caveats I should still wish to enter against it[1]) catches the spirit of the new Reformation on the doctrinal front. He accurately describes the 'difference between us and our ancestors' when he writes:[2]

> We are saying that it is possible today to be agnostic about 'other-worldly' powers and beings, but that people matter, that we live in a world in which 'I' is not 'you' and neither is completely assimilable to 'it' or even to 'he'. We are urging that Buber's distinction matters more than distinctions between eternity and time, infinity and finite, and many other distinctions that mattered to Christians in another age.

And he boldly counters, by acceptance, the charge that this is a 'reduction' of classical theology:[3]

> If this is a reduction in the content of theology, it is the sort of reduction which has been made by modern culture in many fields. Astrology has been 'reduced' to astronomy, for example; we have excluded from the study of the stars a cosmological or metaphysical theory about their effect on human life. Alchemy was 'reduced' to chemistry by the rigorous application of an empirical method. During the Renaissance, the metaphysical ideas and purposes of medieval painting were excluded, leaving 'only' the work of art. In almost every field of human learning, the meta-

[1] See *The Honest to God Debate*, pp. 249-53.
[2] P. 195.   [3] P. 198.

physical and cosmological aspect has disappeared and the subject matter has been 'limited' to the human, the historical, the empirical. Theology cannot escape this tendency if it is to be a serious mode of contemporary thought.

I shall have occasion to return to this fundamental theme of pure theology. But, finally, a preliminary word about what a new Reformation might mean for the organization of the Church.

Stripping of the Structures

The previous Reformation resulted in a gigantic proliferation of structure. As the Body of Christ split up, the separate parts took on the character of the whole. A cluster of little catholicisms was born, each reproducing the characteristics of the parent, with its own ministry and sacraments, its own buildings and budgets. From it we have inherited our present pattern of parallel denominations and overlapping networks of world-wide confessions. We are so used to it that we can readily be persuaded that it has always been so. In fact it is an abomination in church history peculiar, one would like to hope, to the era of the first Reformation. It is surely now on its way out, though it will doubtless be centuries before it disappears. Everything is tending in that direction, and the prayers and actions of all Christians must be engaged in furthering the movements towards organic unity at every level.

But this will not of itself add up to the new Reformation. The process of reunification could simply mean a shortening of the lines, a contracting of the Church's perimeter, and a hardening of the shell. It could strengthen the Church against the world rather than release it for the world. And this indeed is what I fear if the biblical, liturgical and ecumenical movements of our time are *not* accompanied by a new Reformation.

It so happens that as I was preparing this I read in the paper that the average *expenses* allowance of an English diocesan bishop (of whom I am not one!) is £70 a week. This strikes the average Englishman as a great deal of money. In fact, like most figures, it is very misleading and does not represent 'expense account' living but the cost of running his entire office. In terms of wages bills it is modest and adds up to an outlay for which the Church gets more value than from many of its expenditures. Nevertheless, the image remains of a Church remarkably well protected for its mission of being the servant of the world.

The real trouble is not in fact that the Church is too rich but that it has become heavily institutionalized, with a crushing investment in maintenance. It has the characteristics of the dinosaur and the battleship. It is saddled with a plant and a programme beyond its means, so that it is absorbed in problems of supply and preoccupied with survival. The inertia of the machine is such that the financial allocations, the legalities, the channels of organization, the attitudes of mind, are all set in the direction of continuing and enhancing the *status quo*. If one wants to pursue a course which cuts across these channels, then most of one's energies are exhausted before one ever reaches the enemy lines.

There is no easy answer to this—and the more one is involved in the machine, as I am, the more one sees how impossible it is simply to put it into reverse or to start anything from scratch. To get to where you want to go, you have got to begin from where you are. Nevertheless, a new Reformation implies a springtide in the Church, and with it a spring-clean. And such is what Bonhoeffer envisaged in the last chapter of the book he planned but never lived to write:[1]

> The Church is her true self only when she exists for humanity. As a fresh start she should give away all her endowments to the poor and needy. The clergy should live solely on the free-will offerings of their congregations, or possibly engage in some secular calling. She must take her part in the social life of the world, not lording it over men, but helping and serving them. She must tell men, whatever their calling, what it means to live in Christ, to exist for others.

[1] *Op. cit.*, p. 180.

To live for others means to accept life on their terms, to serve within the structures in which they live. The basic trouble is not that the Church has been too affluent—it is chronically short of money—but that it has used it on building its own structures (literally or metaphorically) rather than on serving in those of others. It has been an institution alongside, not the leaven within, the world it exists to change. Perhaps it can only hope to minister to that world by cutting down drastically on its own professionalism (by which I do not mean its own efficiency). I suspect that we should ordain fewer, rather than more, full-time professional clergy on the pay-roll of the Church. And I am sure that we could do with a great deal less ecclesiastical plant. We have got to relearn that 'the house of God' is primarily the world in which God lives, not the contractor's hut set up in the grounds. As Albert van den Heuvel of the Youth Department of the World Council of Churches put it in a lecture on 'the Humiliation of the Church',[1] 'Taking the form of a slave means to let the world have its own forms and fill those with the content of the gospel. Therefore sociology is essential for the Church—it is not helpful, it is essential. Without it we cannot renew our structures. It describes the house in which the slave lives.'

In the words of one of the younger clergy from my own diocese,[2] the 'parish priest is lumbered with parochial machinery designed for fighting, or at least standing over against, the secular front. There is very little machinery available to him for responding to it.' And he went on to describe what a church might look like which was really based on 'the units of our community' rather than on units of ecclesiastical plant. Normally it would simply meet where people are—in the home, the factory, the office or the school.

> On festival occasions such as Christmas, Easter and Whitsun the community centre, a school, or church school would be booked for special gatherings of all Christians in the community.

[1] In the same conference referred to on p. 14.
[2] Christopher Byers, 'Secularization and the Parochial Machine', *Prism*, February 1964, pp. 18-21.

This should not prove difficult to arrange years in advance. Baptisms would be held once or twice a year. Confirmation, like Ordination, would take place in the cathedral of the diocese. The cathedral might serve the role of providing the 'temple element' within the Christian tradition, and would provide visible links with the past heritage of the Church (that should not prove difficult!), as well as with the Church across the world.

All the plant that might be needed locally is a well-equipped parish office with a good shop window—and, of course, houses for community-leaders, ordained and lay. There is not a straight either-or between this and our traditional set-up, and there can be no question in most places of starting again from scratch. But I cite this as an indication of the *direction* in which all our thinking may have to move, even in the responsible administration of our present plant.

Once more this process of stripping down, of travelling light, is not a sign of retreat or a cause for depression. Perhaps I could end by quoting again (I cited it in my essay in *The Honest to God Debate*) a piece of writing which, together with the letter from 'Tertius' quoted by Alec Vidler in *Soundings*,[1] I should like to think might become a psychological (I will not say spiritual) classic of the new Reformation. It is Monica Furlong writing in the English newspaper *The Guardian*[2] (two months, incidentally, before the publication of *Honest to God*):

> The best thing about being a Christian at the moment is that organized religion has collapsed. I know, of course, that the Vatican Council meets, that in churches and chapels up and down the land people are still meeting to worship God, that the splendid farce of established religion still continues, and that the Mothers' Union continues unabashed.
>
> I am deeply involved in formal religion myself, owe it an overwhelming debt, and am only brash enough to scoff at it 90 per cent of the time. But for those who have ears to hear and lips to tell, it is common knowledge that the foundations have shivered, that there are cracks a mile wide in the walls, that the hot ashes

[1] Pp. 247-50.
[2] 11 January 1963. See her subsequent book, *With Love to the Church* (Hodder and Stoughton, London, 1965).

are falling like rain upon our piety, and that the lava is curling about our sacred objects. When we try to walk in the old paths of religion we find them broken and obliterated.

Chacun à son gout, of course, but I cannot imagine a more enjoyable time to be a Christian, except possibly in the first few centuries of the Church. For while the great holocaust is sweeping away much that is beautiful and all that is safe and comfortable and unquestioned, it is relieving us of mounds of Christian bric-à-brac as well, and the liberation is unspeakable. Stripped of our nonsense we may almost be like the early Christians painting their primitive symbols on the walls of the catacombs—the fish, the grapes, the loaves of bread, the cross, the monogram of Christ—confident that in having done so they had described the necessities of life.

If that is what she calls 'the new mutation' in Christianity, I can only say (with much fear and trembling), 'Amen. Come, Lord Jesus.'

The same air of suppressed excitement can be felt today even in the Eternal City. Looking forward from the second session of the second Vatican Council, Michael Novak concludes his brilliant study[1] with the words:

> Old patterns are dissolving. In such a time, the Spirit's activity is almost tangible. . . . The jesters of the fountains smile and say, 'This, too, shall pass', but meanwhile an age of creativity has begun.

It would be wrong, however, to draw the conclusion that this means a return to the catacombs, a withdrawal of the Church from the centres of influence, a reversion to the position of the primitive Christians, who were simply responsible to power but not for it. The Church, of course, may be forced to that position: it may be edged out of the world, like its Master. But deliberately to seek such withdrawal is a failure of responsibility. That is why I am convinced that a church should not *seek* disestablishment. It may have seemed perhaps that the stripping down I have been urging would incline me to advocate

[1] *The Open Church* (Macmillan, New York, and Darton, Longman and Todd, London, 1964).

disestablishment. But that is because establishment is instinctively associated with privilege. In so far as this is the case—and it is—I would agree that the Church must show itself utterly indifferent to it. In fact, however, for the Church of England at any rate, establishment, while it brings a certain prestige, is more of a handicap than a help.[1] In terms of its internal freedom, disestablishment would be a great gain; and I would certainly wish to see a radical reform of the establishment to give the Church in England (comprehending in due course the Methodists and others) the proper self-government enjoyed by the national Church of Scotland.

But establishment itself is not incompatible with the role of the servant. In fact it can be the truest structural expression of it. When the Church has an external relation to the state, there is the greater temptation for it to build its own independent institutions, instead of serving in the house of another. Theologically, too, there is for the Christian no antithesis between the role of the Servant and that of the King. Paul Tillich, after a penetrating discussion of the priestly and prophetic relationships of the Church to society, goes on to insist that, like its Master, it also has its royal office.[2] No position can be, or has been, so easily abused. But this does not release the Servant from responsibility. 'As the royal function belongs to the Christ Crucified, so the royal function must be exercised by the Church under the Cross, the humble church.' It is fully compatible with the proper humiliation of the Church. Indeed, as Tillich reminds us, it is when the Church, to retain its privileges, 'is forced to assume the role of an obedient servant of the state' that we see the other 'humiliation of the church which is not the humility of the Crucified but the weakness of the disciples who fled the Cross'.

---

[1] One of its most restricting handicaps is its inability to determine—as it can with priests—the number of bishops it needs for its pastoral work, quite apart from who chooses them. The freedom to consecrate suffragan or assistant bishops (where the choice of the Crown is already purely formal) could be a first reform.

[2] *Systematic Theology*, vol. iii (University of Chicago Press, 1963, and Nisbet, London, 1964), pp. 212-16.

Only from the Cross can the resurrection of the Church begin. And so I would end with a question. It links the willingness of the Church to surrender its worldly security and emerge from behind its expensive façades with our earlier discussion of the doctrine it can preach. It is this:

> Do we affirm the Easter faith in our time by insisting that God raised Jesus from the dead or by daring to risk ourselves in the confidence that God will raise us from the dead? Can we do the former without the latter?[1]

Again, it is not an either-or. But it is a matter of the way in. And this leads into the fundamental question of the next chapter, of where, in the period of the new Reformation, we can start theologically, if we are to communicate the Gospel *as gospel* at all.

[1] C. Ebb Mundun in *Motive*, January 1963, quoted by Colin W. Williams, *Where in the World?* (National Council of the Churches of Christ in the USA, New York, 1963, and Epworth Press, London, 1965), p. 58.

2

STARTING FROM THE OTHER END

The Gracious Neighbour

LET me begin this chapter with a quotation, which catches, I think, the measure of difference between the old Reformation and the new. It comes from a pioneer evangelist of our time, Horst Symanowski,[1] whose work as an industrial chaplain lies with the religionless working-classes of Western Germany. Previously, he says, the basic problem confronting man was:

> 'How can I find a gracious God?' This question drove men to search desperately for an answer. It was the motor for their action in the world; it unleashed crusades and wars. This cry robbed them of sleep. Do many men lie awake in order to find an answer to this question? We no longer ask this question, or we label it antiquated. But a different question haunts us also. It agitates entire nations. It makes us in our turn victims of anxiety and despair. How can I find a gracious neighbour? How can we still somehow live at peace with one another?[2]

There lies the difference. The old Reformation revolved around Luther's agonized question and his triumphant, liberating answer: 'By faith alone!' It released to men a gracious God. It began from revelation, and centred characteristically in the doctrine of election. And this, for that age, was pure gospel. As the Thirty-Nine Articles put it, ecstatically:

---

[1] *Gegen die Weltfremdheit* (Kaiser Verlag, Munich, 1960), p. 19. Quoted from T. O. Wedel, *The Gospel in a Strange, New World* (Westminster Press, Philadelphia, 1963), p. 40. The whole book is now available in translation by George H. Kehm, *The Christian Witness in an Industrial Society* (Westminster Press, Philadelphia, 1964, and Collins, London, 1965).

[2] Dr Martin Niemöller tells me that precisely the same point was made in his hearing by Pastor Gustav von Bodelschwingh to a group of young pastors as far back as 1924.

STARTING FROM THE OTHER END

'The godly consideration of Predestination, and our Election in Christ, is full of sweet, pleasant, and unspeakable comfort' (Article XVII). And the Church, the company of the elect, was the visible agent and locus of this gospel—'a congregation of faithful men, in the which the pure Word of God is preached, and the Sacraments . . . duly ministered' (Article XIX). Here was the offer. If men passed it by, it could only be to their own damnation.

What has happened? Somehow in the interval the whole ground has shifted. There are, indeed, those who believe that the old word has still to be proclaimed and that this is the simple and unchanged function of the Church. And I would not dream of denying that it can come with power. But this 'positivism of revelation', as Bonhoeffer called it, speaks, I believe, to fewer and fewer, whether in doctrine or in morals. If we say in effect 'Take it or leave it', they leave it. And if we content ourselves with saying that at any rate we have 'preached the Gospel', 'whether they hear or whether they forbear', we shall find it increasingly difficult to carry conviction even with ourselves.

For the fact remains that to larger and larger numbers of our generation *this is simply not gospel*, it evokes no sense of good news, however purely the Word is preached and however duly the Sacraments are administered. And a Church which is identified with this function becomes progressively more irrelevant. For the world is not asking 'How can I find a gracious God?' It *is* asking 'How can I find a gracious neighbour?'[1] And it is starting, not from 'the elect people of God', but from what the most representative collection of photographs of our time called 'the family of man'. It begins, not from revelation, in which it has no prior confidence, but from

[1] Naturally, this is not the *only* question it is asking. There are many whose questionings start from nature rather than from history (witness the remarkable response to Teilhard de Chardin, and L. Charles Birch, *Nature and God* (SCM Press, London, and Westminster Press, Philadelphia, 1965). But in any case the concern is basically one for *meaning* in an apparently hostile universe. See Tillich's substitute for Luther's question, *op. cit.*, iii, p. 227.

relationships, which it is prepared to treat with a greater seriousness than any generation before it. It suspects deductive certainties presented with authority: it respects the validity of convictions, in science or in life, attained inductively from the evidence of experience.

How *in this situation* is the Gospel of Christ to be preached and what is the place of the Church? Is it possible for Christians to accept this shift in the entire frame of reference—and not to sell out? This, I believe, is a very big question, the biggest question for the future of Christianity in our day. I should be foolish if I returned a confident or a simple answer. All I can do is to push through to where I believe the answer is to be sought. It is certain that my version of it will not be adequate; but I shall be content if, instead of pouncing on its inadequacies, others will try to pick up the ball where I drop it and press on.

Fundamentally I believe that we can and must accept the new starting-point. In other words, we must recognize the fact that man's question is *in the first instance* a question about man and not about 'God'—a word which is becoming increasingly problematic to our generation and which has to be 'brought in' more and more unnaturally into any discussion.

To say this will in itself appear to many sufficient evidence of a 'sell-out'. 'Need we call further witnesses? You have heard the blasphemy.'[1] But I would urge a stay of execution. I am *not* suggesting an abandonment of the Christian gospel nor a substitution for it of a pure humanism. Neither am I proposing simply to turn my back on a theology of revelation and replace it with a 'natural theology' which begins with the presuppositions of human nature and hopes to arrive at Christianity from them. That would be to go back on all that my generation in theology has learnt. It is not for nothing that we have been to school with Karl Barth and Emil Brunner and Reinhold Niebuhr. Indeed, if there is a phrase which provides a bridge across into the theology I am concerned to advocate it is Karl

[1] Mark 14.63-4.

Barth's own recent title, 'the humanity of God'.[1] There is nothing further from its spirit than an air of self-confident humanism. Its call is rather to go with Christ outside the camp, to be with him in his humiliation.

For this theology starts from *Christ* as the way into the Father. Indeed, if any text proves central to the new Reformation, as Luther's *sola fide* was to the old, I predict that it will be John 14.9: 'He who has seen me has seen the Father.' For this is its point of entry. To talk about 'God' may, to many, be meaningless; to ask, with Philip, 'Show us the Father' may appear a futile metaphysical question. But all the old questions of *theology* can find their focus and come to rest in this *man*.

But we cannot stop there. For it is not enough to say, 'He who has seen *me* has seen the Father'. This generation goes on to ask the further and equally biblical question: 'But, Lord, when did we see you?'[2] And the answer to that question is given, in the classic 'parable' of the Sheep and the Goats, in terms of the Son of Man *incognito*—in other words, in terms of the 'gracious neighbour'. If men are to see Christ, and therefore God, they can only do it through the one who comes to them, in the first instance, not as a messianic figure, but as one of themselves, as Fred or Harry or the man across the street.

This I believe to be of normative importance for our generation. Reinhold Niebuhr in his Gifford Lectures[3] distinguished between cultures in which a Christ is expected and those in which a Christ is not expected. Using his distinction in a slightly different way, I believe that we must designate ours a post-Christian era, in the sense that a Christ is *no longer* expected. Our generation finds itself in the position of those on the Emmaus road who look back, some with genuine regret,

---

[1] A collection of essays (Collins, London, and John Knox Press, Richmond, Virginia, 1961) widely regarded as an epitomy of 'the later Barth'.
[2] Matthew 25.37-9, 44.
[3] *The Nature and Destiny of Man*, vol. ii (Scribner, New York, and Nisbet, London, 1943), ch. I.

at the Jesus of history as the one who *might have been* the Christ. They ask 'Why should we see in this historical character the focus of all our hopes or the answer to all our problems? Perhaps for another age that was possible. For us, it is no longer so. We are not looking for a Messiah, a single figure who will deliver the world of all its troubles.' They are unable to recognize Jesus as the Christ—for they are not expecting such a manifestation of meaningfulness either for their world or for their lives. And in fact on the Emmaus road he does not confront the couple on their walk as the Christ, but simply as the stranger who comes alongside them in their questioning and their sadness. It is only from there, as the man for others and with others, that he can make himself known to them as the Messiah of whom their Scriptures spoke.

I suspect I am not alone in finding in this story, as in the parable of the Sheep and the Goats and in the final appearance of Jesus to his disciples by the lake-side in John 21, passages of peculiarly compelling power for our generation. For they all tell of one who comes unknown and uninvited into the human situation, disclosing himself as the gracious neighbour before he can be recognized as Master and Lord. And with these passages I would link the story of the Foot-washing in John 13, where, even to those who call him Lord and Master, he can make known the meaning of that lordship only by becoming the servant of all. Together they speak of a *way into* the truth as it is in Jesus which I believe has distinctive significance for our age.[1] It is indeed central to the Christian revelation for any age. For the very meaning of the Incarnation is that the divine enters through the stable door of ordinary human history and everyday experience. It was only in man and as man that men could come to see the Son of God. Indeed, even in a situation that was expecting a Messiah, Jesus clearly found the title 'Christ' as much of an embarrassment as a help. He acknowledged it from the lips of others, but for himself preferred to move among his contemporaries simply as

---

[1] See also W. Hamilton, *The New Essence of Christianity*, chapter III.

'the Son of Man', carrying no celestial credentials, and with nowhere to lay his head.[1]

Perhaps the primary task of theology and of the Church in our generation could be described as making such a meeting possible again. For the effect of the Church's work has been to strip the Christ of his incognito. It has placarded him to men as the Son of God without allowing them to meet him as the Son of Man. It has said to men: 'We have the Christ, defined in our creeds, present in our churches, speaking with final authority in our codes. *Come* to him there. Acknowledge him as Lord and as God.' It has been a deductive rather than an inductive approach, presenting them from the start with the answers they must accept if they are to believe. They have not been called to work out the sum for themselves, to discover the authority *in* the experience, the revelation *in* the relationship, as the first disciples had to before, and again after, the Resurrection. Men of our time, trained in an empirical, scientific discipline, are requiring again to see before they can believe. If they are to acknowledge Jesus as 'the way, the truth and the life', as the definition and vindication of life for them, they must discover him as such '*in* the way'. They must be met by the truth *where they are*—which is largely outside 'the elect

---

[1] Precisely, of course, what Jesus meant by the term Son of Man is a question of debate among New Testament scholars which will presumably never be closed. Suffice it to say that I suspect that it was a term that he deliberately preferred *because* it was open-ended and served as a 'parable' which could be interpreted at different levels. I am not persuaded that for Jesus it had the connotation of the purely celestial apocalyptic figure to be found in the Similitudes of Enoch (the dating of this B.C. is in any case a very open question). In the trial scene (Mark 14.62 and parallels) it certainly carries the associations of Daniel 7.13; but there 'one like a son of man' (i.e. a human being, in contrast with the previous beasts) is an earthly figure, representing the people of God vindicated before him out of suffering and oppression. In general on the lips of Jesus it seems to me to *start* from its basic Hebrew meaning of 'a man' (as in Psalm 8.4; Ezekiel 2.1 *et passim*; cf. Mark 2.27-8; 3.28), with the particular associations of God's true poor man, who, claiming nothing for himself and being reduced to nothing but his bare humanity, is shown to be 'the man of God's right hand' (cf. Psalm 80.17) through whom it is the divine will that our humanity should be judged and restored. The paradox is summed up in the irony of John 19.5: 'Behold the man!'

people of God'—and as the answer to the question *they are asking*—which takes its start from the gracious neighbour rather than the gracious God.

Inductive Faith

In the last of my three lectures in *Christian Morals Today*[1] I tried to explore what this inductive approach 'from the other end' could mean in the field of Christian ethics—where the 'take it or leave it' authoritarian approach is most obviously failing to convince, and those who espouse it are in greatest of danger of being left to the ghetto. I will not repeat here what I tried to say there. I would simply stress the crucial importance of this front. For most doctrinal questions today, in contrast with the period of the previous Reformation, present themselves in the first instance as moral questions. As in the first generation, Christianity is again for our contemporaries being judged primarily as 'the Way', and if it seems irrelevant as this men will not stay to test its claims to be the truth or to bother with the Church.

But I would like to press on to consider the implications of this start from the other end both for the formulation of Christian truth and for the function of the Church.

Let me bring it down to flesh and blood. Just before Easter 1964 I invited to a week-end at our diocesan training centre a group of some of the many people who had written to me over the past year. They represented a cross-section of those to whom the Church as it at present exists appears to have no hooks for their eyes. They were either 'insiders' hanging on because to come out would have seemed the greater betrayal, or 'outsiders' who would have liked to be in but felt that to do so would have meant denying too much in themselves which they knew to be true. Or they were Christians who had given up more than occasional church services because they knew their limitations and found that their faith, hope and charity were just not strong enough! In any case, they were those for

[1] SCM Press, London, and Westminster Press, Philadelphia, 1964.

whom a reiteration of the old Reformation (or Counter-reformation) certainties would merely have widened the gulf. Out of this highly critical and stimulating group two things emerged which for me were to some extent a surprise, and they can serve to introduce the themes I have mentioned.

The first was the vehemence with which almost everyone reacted against the traditional credal and liturgical formulae. And this was not simply a protest against a Church with set forms. There was no evidence that the Free Churches filled the bill any better. In fact if anything they seemed even more washed up. I was taken aback by this vehemence, because on the whole it seems to me that my generation of clergy does not stumble at these in the way in which, say, our predecessors of the twenties and thirties found their faith strained by them. I suppose we all make our private discounts and transpositions, and, with the accepted liberty of interpretation, find them usable, and indeed valuable, as shorthand expressions of the Church's faith and worship. Certainly I am not one of those in the Church of England who want to spend time and energies revising the Thirty-Nine Articles. My brothers in the Protestant Episcopal Church of America seem to me to have chosen the better way, of viewing these as a classic statement of Anglicanism in terms of the previous Reformation and then sitting relatively light to them—though not all perhaps would be prepared to go as far as Bishop James Pike when he says: 'Generally the Articles are simply regarded as the allergic reaction of the Anglican Church, in a particularly trying period, to the fact of "Papists" on the one side and Puritans on the other'![1] Nor, in *Honest to God*, did I find myself wanting to knock the Creeds or the Liturgies as though these represented an intolerable prison house for modern man. On the contrary, I wanted to help him to make the transposition which could enable him to *use* this language and enter into this heritage.

The vehemence, therefore, of these highly intelligent people

[1] *A Time for Christian Candor* (Harper and Row, New York, 1964), p. 30.

against the classic definitions of the Church rather took me aback. As I reflect on it—and it was reinforced by an exactly similar reaction at a second such group—I suspect it represents a deep-seated resistance to any attempt to start from given truths, to prescribe the definition in advance of the experience, the believing ahead of the seeing. For men today cannot see Jesus as the Son of God until they have seen him as the Son of Man. And this is apparently what the Church makes it impossible for them to do. One of the group had said to me on first meeting: 'All the Church seems to have to say to me is, "Come to Evensong and stand up and say the Creed", and this I feel I neither want to nor can.' As a divorced person, this woman was in fact seeking in Christ the gracious neighbour: as a pre-condition she was being offered him as the gracious God. The Church was simply not starting at the end where she was. And, contrary to its own Scriptures, it *gives the impression* of being more interested in hearing the confession 'Lord, Lord' than in making sure that somehow he *does* meet people as 'the man for others'.

Doctrine is the definition of the experience; the revelation discloses itself as the depth and meaning of the relationship. To ask men to believe in the doctrine or to accept the revelation before they see it for themselves as the definition of their experience and the depth of their relationship, is to ask what to this generation, with its schooling in an empirical approach to everything, seems increasingly hollow. In all this frontier-debate I have been made aware that about the one Church in Britain whose public 'image' is not a positive liability is the Society of Friends. And I believe this is because it appears to men to respect this order. I could not myself go with it in rejecting creeds and sacraments, liturgies and ordinations. I believe that these have their rightful place, and I have myself been duly exasperated by the woolliness of the Quakers at their worst! But I am convicted by the integrity which they *seem* to men to have. I have no evidence that they are in fact less hypocritical than the rest of us. But they do not present the impression that the results are prescribed. And I believe it to be a prerequisite of the search in our day that the ends should genuinely be open.

As a convinced Christian I may be persuaded that the path cannot finally stop short of the confession: 'My Lord and my God!'[1] But I am sure that most of my generation have got to come to it in the way St Thomas did, out of the fires of experience, and that to require of them in advance a definition for which they are not ready is bound to have the same effect as it would have had on him.

Let me illustrate. One of the things that presents a major stop in the mind for our generation is the *uniqueness* of Christ. Of course, this is nothing new. It is an integral part of the 'offence' of the Gospel. Men have always stumbled at the 'scandal of particularity'—and never more than in a society which is conditioned by all its historical and scientific training to see the particular as but one instance of the general. But I get the impression that it is being made peculiarly and unnecessarily difficult by being presented as an objective fact to be swallowed at the beginning of the search. Men have Christ set before them as what appears to them a unique *kind* of being—half God and half man, quite different from the rest of us—whom they simply have to accept as such as part of 'Christian doctrine'. But, starting from the inductive end, I can only *begin* with the statement that Christ is a perfectly ordinary human being ('very man' in traditional terms) who is *unique for me*, in the sense that in him 'all things cohere':[2] he is the one who co-ordinates and vindicates for me all that I believe most deeply true, in the way that Mahommed or Buddha does not. I can say with the early Church, 'Jesus is Lord', or with Thomas, 'My Lord and my God'. And I can go on to spell that out in terms of the Creeds, that this is the one who is the unique expression of God in human life ('the only begotten Son of the Father'). But I am more concerned that people should be able to set their foot on the path (and feel accepted for doing so) than with whether they have reached the end of it (and feel rejected for not having done so).

[1] John 20.28. [2] Colossians 1.17.

This inductive approach to Christian doctrine is, I am convinced, a discipline which the Church has got to re-learn. It is not conceived out of any desire to water down the faith. It does not prescribe the ends negatively. But it does insist that the ends are only to be reached from the beginning—and the beginning for men today, as for the first disciples, is from Jesus as a completely human man[1]—*whatever more they may be compelled to see in him*. Indeed, I suspect that for our generation, 'a completely human man' is a better translation of the Greek *teleios* than 'a perfect man'. For the Church has succeeded in presenting the sinless perfection of Christ in a way that has failed to convince modern, Darwinian, Freudian, man that he could have been *completely* human. And for that reason contemporary man is inclined, understandably, to dismiss him as a possible definition, let alone as the unique definition, of a genuinely human existence.

It is a question of the way in. If, say, the Virgin Birth is presented as the precondition of a Christian estimate of Jesus (and that is what most non-Christians think it is), then its effect, so far from establishing his divinity, will be to make men query his humanity. If one starts with his indisputable humanity, as the disciples did, then one may be able to see that what the birth narratives are attempting is to interpret, in the language of their age, the *significance* of this human life: it is fully understandable only as it is as grounded in a much

---

[1] By this I certainly do not mean, as the Liberal Protestants of an earlier generation tended to mean, that people must be enabled to meet the pre-resurrection 'Jesus of history' stripped of the 'accretions' of the 'Christ of faith'. It is the Christ 'according to the Spirit' who is alone our contemporary. I would not for one minute deny the necessity and the power of the Jesus of history, which those who first accepted the Christ of faith themselves insisted on by writing not only Epistles but Gospels. But for men to meet Jesus as the definition and vindication of *their* humanity—to see him as *the* Son of Man—they must, as in the Gospels, meet him incarnate, in the Son of Man *on earth*. And he is thus earthed not primarily in words (even in those of the Gospels) but in flesh—in the least of his brethren, whether confessedly in those who acknowledge him or unconfessedly in those whom he acknowledges. The task therefore of the Church is to *be* this Son of Man on earth, allowing its imperfect incarnation to be judged constantly by *the* Incarnation. And for this latter the Gospels are irreplaceable.

deeper cause than 'the fleshly desire of a human father'.[1] And that significance is independent of how physically or metaphysically, historically or mythologically, individual Christians may take the stories—on which they may legitimately differ.

Or, take the closely connected doctrine of the pre-existence of Christ. As a precondition, again, of a Christian estimate, it seems to many to commit them in advance to a proposition for which they have, and could have, no conceivable evidence. If this is a requirement of the package deal, it appears to many honest people to disqualify them in advance. In any case, it actually hinders rather than helps them to start where the disciples did—with Jesus as a completely ordinary human being. To use a piece of theological shorthand, their point of contact and departure is the pro-existence of Jesus, the one who exists *for* others, not his pre-existence.

What the New Testament is doing with this further language is to ask the *significance* of this Man for others. Is he just a 'sport', a biological accident? Is he simply of interest in himself as an individual, or for the contemporaries who happened to meet him? Or does he point to some deeper universal truth about our humanity? Is he in some sense a definition for all men of what a genuinely human existence should be? Is the revelation he embodies as to 'what is in man' something that just happened to surface at that moment of history, or does it tell us more of the ground and meaning of all history? It is with such probing questions that the early Christians recorded on Jesus' lips the mysterious phrase, 'Before Abraham was, I am',[2] or came to view his earthly life in terms of predestination (if they were Jews) or in terms of pre-existence (if they were Greeks). But all these were theological explorations—registering convictions thrown up by experience and starting from his humanity. And this is the door which the Church must make it more obviously possible for men to enter today. Where they go from there must be a matter of *trust*, not of predefinition.

I am increasingly persuaded that the churches (and the Church of England in particular, which alone in Christendom

[1] John 1.13. [2] John 8.58.

prescribes the Athanasian Creed for public worship—though mercifully it is obsolescent) appear to place far too much insistence on the recitation of formulae and declarations of assent. Let the historic creeds and confessions be there, in the way that title-deeds and constitutions are, but let us not constantly be straining men's loyalty, sincerity and understanding by asking them to take them upon their lips or to sign on the dotted line. I would gladly see subscription to the Thirty-Nine Articles abolished, as it has been in other parts of the Anglican Communion without disaster or loss of definition. When we need public affirmations of belief (and like confessions we can overdo them), let us have simple, untechnical ones. And let them begin with 'We' not 'I'. For this reflects much more accurately the status (and the confidence) of public proclamation as opposed to (the varying degrees of) private dedication.

Tillich seems to me to sum up the situation with great insight and sympathy when he writes:[1]

> A church is a community of those who affirm that Jesus is the Christ. The very name 'Christian' implies this. For the individual, this means a decision—*not* as to whether he, personally, can accept the assertion that Jesus is the Christ, *but* the decision as to whether he wishes to belong or not to a community which asserts that Jesus is the Christ. If he decides against this, he has left the church, even if, for social or political reasons, he does not formalize his denial. Many formal members in all the churches more or less consciously do not want to belong to the church. The church can tolerate them, because it is not based on individual decisions but on the spiritual Presence and its media.
>
> In the opposite situation, there are some who unconsciously or consciously want to belong to the church, and who are in a state of such doubt about the basic assertion that Jesus is the Christ and its implications that they are on the verge of separating themselves from the church, at least inwardly. In our time, this is the predicament of many people, perhaps even the majority, though in various degrees. They belong to the church, but they doubt whether they belong. For them it must be said that the

[1] *Systematic Theology*, vol. iii, pp. 174-5.

criterion of one's belonging to a church and through it to the spiritual community is the serious desire, conscious or unconscious, to participate in the life of a group which is based on the New Being as it has appeared in Jesus as the Christ. Such an interpretation can help people whose consciences are troubled by misgivings about the whole set of symbols to which they subject themselves in thought, devotion and action. They can be assured that they fully belong to the church, and through it to the Spiritual Community, and can confidently live in it and work for it.

But there are many who feel themselves to be still further out than this and have no wish to be 'assured that they fully belong' when they know they do not. They are like the 'god-fearers' of ancient Judaism who knew they could not accept the yoke of circumcision and the Law and yet whom Israel attracted rather than repelled—a grace to which the new Israel seems to find it so hard to give structure. Their desire is to be accepted not as full members, acknowledging the faith and order of a particular church, but as guests. Of these Tillich says:

> Such situations are frequent today. What is decisive, at least in the Protestant sphere, is the desire to participate in a group whose foundation is the acceptance of Jesus as the Christ; this desire takes the place of credal statement and, in spite of absence of conversion, opens the door into the community of love without reservation on the side of the church.[1]

Since Tillich specifically says 'at least in the Protestant sphere', it is worth observing that even this reservation, which until recently would have been valid, is now, like so much else, under question. In a recent article in the North American Roman Catholic journal, *The Ecumenist*,[2] Fr Gregory Baum explores a very similar line to Tillich's under the traditional Catholic doctrine of 'the baptism of desire'. Under this notion, he says,

> We may include the vast action of God to save and sanctify

[1] *Op. cit.*, p. 181.
[2] '*Honest to God* and Traditional Theology', May-June 1964, pp. 65-8.

men outside the visible boundaries of the Church. While this baptism, as distinct from the baptism of water, does not introduce men into a believing community in which they are fed by an intimate communion with their God (and hence remains a weak initiation into a reality which is fully present only in the Church) one may seriously wonder whether baptism of desire is not the way of salvation for the great majority of men in this world, chosen to be saved!

Coming from a Roman Catholic, this may reinforce the conviction that the frontier may indeed be open without the centre being sacrificed.

The Accepting Community

This has already led right into the second topic—the function of the Church and its consequent structure. Not only must its theology be open-ended, it must itself be a genuinely open society. In terms of the group of which I spoke this defined itself in the possibility of the Church being and being seen to be the 'accepting community'. Everything for them hinged on this; and the reelvation of the week-end was that perhaps it really could be. The characteristic of such a community is that it is prepared to meet men *where they are* and accept them *for what they are*. And despite the Pauline injunction, 'Accept one another as Christ accepted us',[1] this is not how the Church had in fact presented itself to them. They had seen it, as indeed the Church defined itself, as a 'congregation of faithful men, in which the pure Word of God is preached and the Sacraments ... duly ministered'. And to come from where they were to where that was, to turn from being 'outsiders' to being inside what seemed a closed circle, was not a journey they felt they could make.

The whole tendency of the Reformation-Counter-reformation era was to think of the Church in terms of the gathered or the excommunicating group. It *defined* the Church when it was

[1] Romans 15.7.

out of the world, as the salt piled, clean and white, in the cellar, as the leaven unmixed with the meal. And this is precisely when it is *not* being itself or performing its essential function. For it is distinctively itself when it cannot be seen and tasted for itself at all, but when it is transforming whatever it is in.

I believe that in our age we have got to discover a different pattern or model of the Church to describe its normative mode of existence. For the first Reformation the norm of Christian existence was a community of the elect gathered out of this naughty world and organized as a visible institution within it and over against it. The Church was distinctively itself when it was manifest, separate. It was a circle of light bounded by the world, and a person was either in it or in darkness.

I suggest that the image with which we have to work is somewhat different. There will still be what Tillich has designated the distinction between the 'manifest' church and the 'latent' church (in contrast with the unhappy distinction between the visible and invisible church of the old Reformation). These he has defined as follows:[1] 'The latent church is an indefinite historical group which within paganism, Judaism or humanism actualizes the New Being, while the manifest church is a definite historical group in which the New Being is actualized directly and manifestly.' It corresponds with the distinction I referred to earlier between the Christ acknowledged and the Christ incognito. And 'where Christ is'—*where either Christ is*—'there is the Church'. In its latent form of existence it may not be organized, it may not be able to say 'Lord, Lord', and within it the pure Word of God is certainly not preached nor the Sacraments duly ministered. And yet it may be nearer

---

[1] *Propositions* (unpublished), Part iv, p. 27, quoted in *The Theology of Paul Tillich*, ed. Charles W. Kegley and Robert W. Bretall (Macmillan, New York, 1952), p. 259. I have kept, for convenience, the terms 'latent church' and 'manifest church'. Tillich is still prepared to use them, but in his *Systematic Theology*, vol. iii, pp. 152-7, he prefers to speak of the difference between 'the Spiritual Community in its latency and in its manifestation'. It is noteworthy that he treats what are normally called the 'marks' of the Church (holiness, unity, universality, etc.) as the marks of the Spiritual Community, *latent or manifest*. They are neither unambiguous in the historic churches, nor absent outside them.

the truth to view it as the latent Church than as the godless world.

The picture of Christian mission with which we have hitherto worked has envisaged, as I said, a circle of light (with Christ at its centre), surrounded by a penumbra of 'fringers' and 'outsiders', whom it is the task of the Church to 'visit' and 'bring in'. Their distance from Christ has been directly proportional to their distance from the manifest Church. I believe that this is far too simplified a picture, particularly in our post-Christian situation, where for many the Christ can make himself known *only* if he comes to them incognito, as the gracious neighbour, rather than as the messianic or hieratic figure of the manifest Church. Indeed, it is religious presumption to assume that Christ is in the centre of the Church's circle and not in the dark world. Moreover, the question insistently posed by the Gospels is not how far men are from the manifest Church but how far they are from the kingdom of God.

What then is the function of the manifest Church in the new Reformation? I suggest that it is not there primarily as the organized centre *into* which to draw men—as if the enlarging of this circle were the object of the whole exercise. It is indeed the dedicated nucleus of those who actively acknowledge Jesus as Lord and have committed themselves to membership and mission within the visible sacramental fellowship of the Spirit. Yet its *normal* form of existence, when it is distinctively being itself, is *not* to be gathered together in one place, but to be embedded as seeds of light within the dark world. And, within this world, by no means its only job is to make more Christians, that is, more members of the manifest Church. Yet this is regularly assumed to be the goal to which the whole of the Church's mission is geared. It is taken for granted, both inside and outside the Church, that the eventual, if not the immediate, aim of all it does is to elicit that commitment.

But this I believe needs questioning in the light of the Bible. For while the New Testament holds out as the consummation of all things the vision of *Christ* as all in all, it never suggests

STARTING FROM THE OTHER END

that all men will be in *the Church*, at any rate within this age. In fact, right through to the Book of Revelation, it continues to visualize the covenant people as a minority instrument of the Kingdom. Of the Church alone, it has been said, its 'minority status is not a scandal'.[1]

Perhaps the closest modern parallel is the relationship between the Communist party and the state in Soviet Russia. As is well known, the Communist party is a small minority in Soviet society, and by no means its only function is to make more communists. Without the party the régime would indeed collapse, but its tactics are not based on the assumption that all Russians will become communists, in the sense of acknowledging a conscious ideological commitment and discipline. Its policy is geared to making Russia and eventually the world a socialist society.

To transfer the analogy to the Christian mission, it is possible to regard the 'latent Church' either from the point of view of the 'manifest Church' or from the point of view of the Kingdom of God. Evangelism in modern parlance has come to be seen almost exclusively in the former perspective: it means drawing individuals across the line into the camp of committed Christians. But from many of those for whom the Kingdom 'drew near' in the ministry of Jesus he sought to elicit no such commitment. For the Syrophoenician woman,[2] for instance, the good news of the Kingdom—the Gospel—was precisely that he was able to meet her *where she was*, as the gracious neighbour, in answer to her absolutely elemental human need—despite the fact that she was not even one of the lost sheep of the house of Israel.

Today, I believe, the main work of the manifest Church, certainly in terms of sheer numbers, is probably to make it possible for men and women to be met by Christ *where they are*—that is, within the context and thought-forms of the latent church. It has to ask itself whether what it really cares

---

[1] R. P. McBrien, 'The Church as the Servant of God', *The Clergy Review*, July 1963, p. 413.
[2] Matthew 15.21-8; Mark 7.24-30.

for most is that 'the poor *have* the Gospel preached to them'—if need be in the entirely non-religious terms announced by Jesus, of release for prisoners and recovery of sight for the blind[1]—even if they never say, 'Lord, Lord'. If so, then it must, for the greater part of its work, be prepared to *respect* rather than remove (which is its instinctive urge) the incognitos under which the parable of the Sheep and the Goats alone shows it possible for the Christ to meet and to judge the mass of men.[2] And the incognitos of that parable are those of *humanity* and *secularity*: the Son of Man wills to be met in an utterly disinterested concern for persons for their own sake, and in relationships that have nothing distinctively religious about them.

Now the reaction of the churchman to accepting these incognitos is to say that this is 'reducing' the Gospel to mere humanism and 'giving in' to secularism. This I would strenuously deny. Indeed, I believe that these are the only forms under which it is possible to communicate the things of God to the majority of men and women in our contemporary post-religious world. And in and through these forms I am convinced that the whole Word can still become flesh. After all, it is not for nothing, as I said earlier, that Jesus *preferred* to

[1] Luke 4.18.
[2] The parable speaks in the first instance of the judgment of 'nations' (Matthew 25.32), and while it cannot be so confined I believe it has a particular relevance for the relation of the Gospel to man in the mass. Commenting on another passage ('Go and make disciples of all nations', Matthew 28.19), the World Council of Churches' study, *A Theological Reflection on the Work of Evangelism* (1963), says this: 'The term "nation" is used in sufficiently broad ways in the Bible to warrant its application to peoples in their total linguistic, social, cultural and religious settings. The witness of the Gospel must be made to men as they actually are, within the groupings of nation, community, occupation, culture and religion in which they actually live. The whole structure of meanings found in such groupings is an inseparable part of the lives of those who live and work within them, and must be taken with full seriousness in the missionary task.' I have tried to work this out in relation to the mass-medium of religious television, whose first object, I believe, must *not* be to strip away the incognitos or transfer men from the latent church into the manifest church, but to present Christ within the categories of the latent church ('Communicating with Contemporary Man', in the Report, *Religion in Television*, Independent Television Authority, London, 1964, pp. 27-35).

communicate with his contemporaries simply as 'the Son of Man'.

So often in the past—and indeed in the present—the image of the Church has been an anti-humanist one, both doctrinally and morally. This is true doctrinally, because it has been one of our most deeply ingrained assumptions, reinforced by the previous Reformation, that the Word of God is to be heard in words—whereas the Incarnation should surely have taught us that it is primarily spoken in flesh. The main reason why men have not heard is not the ineffectiveness or the unintelligibility of our words (and I would never under-rate their barrier), but what George MacLeod has called[1] 'our de-humanizing of him who is our sole salvation'. What we have preached to men is not Jesus come, and coming, in the flesh, but a disincarnate Word—doctrinally orthodox, no doubt, but not seen as meeting them out of the eyes of men, women and children.

Morally, too, the Church appears so constantly to the modern world to be in the anti-humanist camp. Time and again it seems to act and speak as though man *were* made for the Sabbath, as though principles were more important than persons, rather than *vice versa*. Unless the Church can really convince men that it is more deeply and honestly interested in persons for their own sake than any of the other humanisms of our day, then I believe it will merely be judged by them— and the standard of judgment will be that of the Son of Man.

Secondly, any presentation of Christianity with a hope of speaking outside the religious in-group must be genuinely and gladly secular. This will doubtless seem merely quixotic to most churchmen, who still speak and write[2] as though 'the Christian mind' and 'the secular mind' were simply antithetical. 'Secular*ism*', like 'scient*ism*', and indeed human*ism*, as a self-contained philosophy, may be a great enemy. But I believe it is of the utmost importance to recognize that secularization itself represents a shift in man's whole way of looking at the

[1] *Only One Way Left* (The Iona Community, Glasgow, 1956), p. 46.
[2] E.g. H. Blamires, *The Christian Mind* (SPCK, London, and Seabury Press, Greenwich, Conn., 1963).

world (such as marked the transition between the Middle Ages and the Renaissance) towards which the Christian faith as such is neutral—if indeed, like the scientific revolution, it is not an actual fruit of the Gospel.[1] In any case, it must be respected and welcomed as the God-given frame of reference within which the Christ has to be made flesh for our day.

Is a 'secular' reinterpretation of the Gospel possible which would permit man today to be a Christian without forcing him to feel that in order to do so he must go back upon the age to which he belongs and embrace the equivalent of a 'medieval' world-view? In other words, 'Can a truly contemporary person be a Christian?' That is the question with which Dr Peter Berger begins *The Precarious Vision*.[2] People are divided, he says, into those who say 'Of course!' and those who say 'Of course not!' Neither answer he thinks will do. He believes the answer is 'Yes—but not of course.' I agree. I am profoundly convinced that a truly contemporary person *can* be a Christian, but not if his acceptance of the Faith is *necessarily* tied to certain traditional thought-forms—metaphysical, supranaturalistic, mythological and religious—against which secularization marks a decisive revolt.[3] And these thought-forms have been so inextricably associated with the presentation of the Christian Gospel that to detach them will not be easy. Yet to go on preaching in them, however viable they may have been, and still are for many, is simply to invite obsolescence.

But let me end this chapter where I began. It is unthinkable that I could wish to change the Gospel or to water it down to make it more palatable. But I am passionately concerned that it shall be able to come to men *as good news*. And to proclaim it from the pulpit, six feet above contradiction, in terms of the gracious God of the old Reformation is not, I am persuaded, going to match that need. But if through the accepting com-

---

[1] See Harvey G. Cox, *The Secular City* (Macmillan, New York, and SCM Press, London, 1965). I have only had the privilege of reading this in manuscript after completing my own. It seems to me a major contribution.
[2] Doubleday, New York, 1961, p. 8.
[3] See *The Honest to God Debate*, esp. pp. 248-75.

STARTING FROM THE OTHER END

munity, whether latent or manifest, men can discover the gracious neighbour, then I am convinced that it will be possible for them to find for themselves all that the Church has ever meant by 'the grace of our Lord Jesus Christ and the love of God and the fellowship of Holy Spirit'.

3

TOWARDS A GENUINELY LAY THEOLOGY

The Lay Church

THE theme of this chapter, as its title implies, is the exploration of what might be meant by a truly 'lay theology'. But it is necessary to begin from 'the theology of the laity'—which is not quite the same thing.

The current renewal of the Church in our day is marked not only by the biblical, liturgical and ecumenical movements but by a great quickening of the laity, a thawing of 'God's frozen people'.[1] In one respect this is simply the outworking of the old Reformation, taking seriously, at last, its rediscovery of the priesthood of all believers and of the freedom, responsibility and ministry of every Christian man. And like the other three streams of renewal, it is not now confined to one side of the Reformation-Counter-reformation divide.[2] Indeed, the very issues which in the sixteenth century divided us—the Bible, the vernacular, the liturgy, the laity—are now bringing Catholic and Protestant together. On these fronts we can gladly go forward side by side and learn from each other.

Nevertheless, this movement of the Spirit, unless it is to encounter frustration, must sooner or later break the bounds of the old Reformation. For the presuppositions of the Reformers' doctrine of the Church were still those of a gathered, settled congregation dominated by a clericalism of the Word, if not of the Sacraments. 'Involving the laity' (or, in the still more tell-tale phrase, 'using the laity') has meant

[1] The title of a book by Mark Gibbs and T. Ralph Morton (Fontana Books, London, 1964, and Westminster Press, Philadelphia, 1965).
[2] See, notably, Fr Y. Congar, O.P., *Lay People in the Church* (translated by Donald Attwater, Chapman, London, 1957) and H. Kraemer, *A Theology of the Laity* (Lutterworth Press, London, 1958).

TOWARDS A GENUINELY LAY THEOLOGY

giving them their place, or even their head, in an institution firmly, if unobtrusively, controlled by the clergy. The typical assumptions of the Reformation church come out in the response, the only response, asked of the congregation in the traditional service for the induction of a new vicar in the Church of England: 'Will you pray continually for this your minister who is set over you in the Lord, and help him forward in all the duties of his holy calling?' The priest has the ministry and the holy calling: the people's responsibility is to *help him*.[1] Indeed, even in so forward-looking a document as Leslie Paul's Report on *The Deployment and Payment of the Clergy* you may still find a sub-heading:[2] 'The Laity to the Help of the Ministry'. Despite the fact, as Kathleen Bliss has reminded us,[3] that at least 99.5 per cent of the Church is not ordained, 'going into the church' and 'entering the ministry' have regularly been confined in popular parlance to ordination.

All this has now been said many, many times, and theoretically at any rate we should most of us be prepared to subscribe to the proposition enunciated by Hans Ruedi Weber of the Department of Laity of the World Council of Churches: 'The laity are not the helpers of the clergy so that the clergy can do their job, but the clergy are helpers of the whole people of God, so that the laity can be the Church.' But any new Reformation is, I suggest, going to demand of us not only a *reversal* of roles for which psychologically we are still unprepared, but even, maybe, an abolition of these roles.

Let me explain what I mean.

I have no doubt whatever that the Church will continue to require diversities of ministry—and indeed a much greater diversity than the few stereotypes to which the Spirit has been confined since the shape of the ministry hardened in the early centuries. I have no doubt too that the Church should ordain, set apart, or otherwise acknowledge with prayer, thanksgiving

[1] Cf., further, my essay 'The Ministry of the Laity' in *Layman's Church*, ed. T. W. Beaumont (Lutterworth Press, London, 1963), pp. 9-22.

[2] Church Information Office, London, 1964, p. 148.

[3] *We the People* (SCM Press, London, 1963, and Fortress Press, Philadelphia, 1964).

and authority, those called and commissioned to special functions in the name of its Head and members. What I question is whether most of the traditional lines of demarcation which run through the ministry of the Church, and which were accepted by the Reformers without serious question, bear any more relation to the battles of tomorrow than the trenches of yesterday's war. In fact they are increasingly becoming a positive hindrance to freedom of manoeuvre.

I do not propose to trace these demarcations in any detail. I had a good straight look at them in a lecture I gave some years ago, called 'Taking the Lid off the Church's Ministry', published in a symposium, *New Ways with the Ministry*.[1] Here let me simply mention them, adding a few subsequent comments.

The first is the basic division between clergy and laity—what I called *the clergy line*—which cuts its way through the diversities of administration within the Church, often arbitrarily but usually quite firmly. This is a line of quite a different nature from those distinguishing the various offices or orders of ministry (bishops, priests, deacons, readers, catechists, etc.) to which the Church under the guidance of the Spirit has from the beginning commissioned its members. It is as though somewhere through the middle of these divisions ran an invisible line, marking off those above from those below the salt. In the Presbyterian Church, for instance, it goes right through the middle of a single order of ministry, dividing the Teaching Elder, who is a clergyman, from the Ruling Elder, who is a layman. In the Church of England the line between clergy and laity is drawn below the diaconate, although in *function* deacons and lay readers are far closer than deacons and priests. Moreover, deaconesses, though in Orders, are not (so it is judged) in Holy Orders: they belong not to the house of clergy but to the house of laity, and this is solemnly stated in the revised Canons to be 'without prejudice to . . . their order'.

We should be ready to recognize that this 'clergy line' is

[1] Ed. John Morris (Faith Press, London, 1960), pp. 9-21.

TOWARDS A GENUINELY LAY THEOLOGY 57

neither native nor essential to the Church. It is indeed an alien importation, introduced from the difference between the *plebs* and the *ordo*, the commons and the senate, in the administrative machinery of the Roman empire. It was entrenched in the Church at the time of its establishment under Constantine, when it became necessary to define the rights and benefits of clergy transferred to it from the heathen priesthood. I believe the whole thing could disappear without loss, together with the medieval concept of indelibility,[1] the mystique, the status, the theology and the legalities by which it has been buttressed and surrounded in our various traditions. The whole differentiation implied in the terms '*sacred* ministry' and '*holy* orders' is one that is now destructive rather than constructive of the Body of Christ. As an unusually outspoken Church of England report put it,[2] 'Many would receive fresh encouragement to be better people in their own spheres if the too-prevalent attitude towards the clergy as the recipients of some semi-magical status could be clearly and forcibly disclaimed, discouraged and discarded.' The old Reformation was compatible with the survival of clericalism, and indeed its reassertion in fresh forms, although it certainly is not scriptural. The new Reformation must see it go, if the whole Body of Christ is really to be released for its ministry to the world.

The second line that must surely go is what I have called *the professional line*, which reserves the ordained ministry, with

[1] This is part of the 'occult' view of life analysed by John Wren-Lewis in his article 'The Decline of Magic in Art and Politics' (*The Critical Quarterly*, Spring 1960, pp. 7-23). Such a view survives also in the legal fiction that the epicopal consecration of a church or graveyard is 'for ever'—a fiction that the Church of England has to spend a disproportionate amount of its time, energies and money voiding or evading. I would like to take a vow never to consecrate a piece of property again (in contrast to dedicating it, which has exactly the same theological significance, but without the magic). But then in the Church of England the church could not legally be a parish church, the house could not be a vicarage, and the living would not qualify for a penny from the Church Commissioners! There are probably more urgent things for which to go to the stake or the poor house.

[2] *Gender and Ministry*, presented to the Church Assembly by the Central Advisory Council for the Ministry (Church Information Office, London, 1962), p. 11.

few exceptions, to those who derive their living from it. Must the priesthood necessarily or normally be a profession? Certainly it was not in the early Church, where this line, again, was non-existent. The financial ability of the Church to free its leadership for full-time duties represented an obvious gain. But the restriction of the priesthood, and in due course the diaconate also, to those extracted from the world's life introduced a line which pastorally, evangelistically and economically is proving increasingly unsatisfactory.

Reacting from the abuses of the Middle Ages, where multitudes of very mundane 'clerks' were in holy orders, the Reformers entrenched the professional line yet further. In fact, it is very difficult to read the Ordinal of the Church of England without seeing it as commissioning a full-time professional clerisy, living by the Gospel. Indeed, the connection between ordination and 'a living', as its natural goal and climax, has bitten deeply into the whole psychology of the Church of England, and with it the baleful effects of another line which I have called 'the great benefice barrier'.[1] This bedevils all questions of mobility, security, salary and status as between those clergy who have 'arrived' and those who have not. It also entrenches the assumption that residential cures (vested in a piece of freehold property) represent the normative, permanent ministry of the Church, to which anything else is purely supplementary. But there is no need here to expatiate on the peculiar—and often amusing—anomalies of the Church of England. In other forms, they can doubtless be paralleled in most of our traditions.

Rather, I should wish to question more fundamentally whether ordination in any of our churches should ever include a built-in guarantee of £1,000 a year for life (or whatever is its equivalent). Ordination means the commissioning of a man for a particular order or function of ministry within the Body of Christ. It need not of itself imply any undertaking that he is to be taken on to the pay-roll of the Church or will remain on it. The Church should remain entirely free in this matter,

[1] *Prism*, December 1963, pp. 4-13.

and make it clear from the beginning that ordination is a calling and not necessarily a profession. Of course, such freedom entails responsibility—the responsibility of seeing, like the Jewish Church of old, that no one is ordained without a trade, the responsibility of cushioning a man against change of employment and loss of housing, especially later in life, and the responsibility of a redundancy, retirement, and if necessary retraining, programme as fair as that of any business firm. But if the Church is to travel sufficiently light, and to be flexible for a mobile society organized on functional lines, then it must be free to deploy much if not most of its manpower not for servicing units of ecclesiastical plant but for serving within the structures of the world.

Thirdly, the Church of the new Reformation must tackle what the old Reformers hardly touched, and what is still too hot for most churchmen, namely, *the sex line*, as it cuts its path through the whole ministry of the Church, ordained and unordained. I am increasingly persuaded that this is not the isolated and secondary issue of ecclesiastical controversy that most of our churches would prefer to keep it. The previous Reformation did nothing to convince women that they were not second-class citizens in the Kingdom of God—except allow them to become clergy wives! Then, no doubt, it did not matter greatly whether they were convinced or not. But now it is vital. Unless the Church can show that it is prepared to permit women as full scope for ministry *and responsibility* as ever it gives to men—and as the world is increasingly giving to women—then it has no right to preach to the world a Gospel which declares that 'in Christ there is neither male nor female'.

This has been borne in upon me by a recent visit to Sweden,[1] where the Church of the old Reformation faces modern secular society in starker contrast than anywhere else I know. There the issue of women-priests merely happens to focus the crisis of secularization which confronts the Church everywhere. It was no accident that the fascinating confrontation of Christians and agnostics for which I was asked over was

[1] I have written more fully on this in *Prism*, April 1964, pp. 36-8.

arranged by their leading woman priest-theologian. I had supposed before that the connection between *Honest to God* and the ordination of women was peripheral. But in Sweden the two are part of the same fight for the ear of twentieth-century society—and, who knows, perhaps elsewhere also? At any rate, just after I returned I happened to receive a letter from a woman author, from which I quote the last paragraph:

> My friends point out that a half-witted man can, for a small instance, take round a collecting bag, but that the most brilliant woman must have no part nor lot in the Church.[1] Even the mild suggestion of making them Lay Readers has met with fanatical resistance. My personal faith is deep-rooted and does not matter, but is there any answer that I can give myself and my sceptical friends? Is there any way of making them see that our God does regard all souls of equal value in spite of the Church, which certainly does not? All clergymen shy away from this, but the comfort and confirmation your book has given offers me a faint hope.[2]

The new Reformation cannot, I am convinced, burke these issues if it is to have a hope of getting off the ground. But it has not only a revolution in the theology of the laity to see through. It has, I believe, the still more far-reaching task of moving towards a genuinely lay theology—which may indeed prove the distinctive contribution of our period to the history of the Church.

A New Setting for Theology

For a point of departure I would turn this time to a Roman Catholic. In a recent article in *The Downside Review*[3] Charles Davis[4] wrote illuminatingly of what he called 'the ecology of

[1] This is clearly an exaggeration. But that no doubt is how it looks and feels.
[2] See the remarkable protest from the Roman Catholic side against the denial of orders to women and its indefensible Thomistic basis by Dr Gertrud Heinzelmann, 'The Place of Women in the Church', *Pax Romana*, 1964, No. 5.
[3] October 1963, pp. 307-16.
[4] Professor of Dogmatic Theology at St Edmund's College, Ware, the seminary of the Archdiocese of Westminster.

theology'. By this he meant the influence of the environment in which theology has been done in different periods and situations in the Church's life. He traces, so far, four different theological 'cultures' in the history of Christendom.

1. 'Theology in the patristic age', he says, 'was predominantly an *episcopal* theology. The leading theologians, such as Athanasius, Basil, Augustine, were bishops, and, even where the theological writings are not the work of bishops, they are strongly marked by the pastoral concern of the Church.' And he sees this type of theology, like all the others, as one of abiding necessity for the life of the Church. 'There is a contribution to theology that can be made only by bishop-theologians. The fact that no bishop, however theologically minded, would bother with some of the questions discussed by theologians would have a purifying effect on theology were bishops more closely involved in theological activity than they are.'

But the distinctive characteristic of this type of theology, as of each of the others, is not primarily *who* does it or *where*, but the thrust and motive-power for it. In this first instance theology is a function of *episcope* or oversight, of feeding, guiding and ruling the flock. It is the kind of theology of which a bishop is charged at his consecration to be the guardian and guarantor. But it certainly is not the exclusive prerogative of bishops. Indeed, most of the historic names in the Church's theology fall naturally into this category—not only Athanasius and Augustine, but Luther and Calvin, Hooker and Wesley, Forsyth and Barth. In the Church of England it has traditionally been pursued, not only or even chiefly in episcopal palaces, but in cathedral closes and country vicarages; and its latest example of such a theology of episcopal care and oversight is the work of a layman, the Report of Mr Leslie Paul on *The Deployment and Payment of the Clergy*. In all our traditions today the most characteristic manifestation of this type of theology is to be seen in the official commission appointed by a denomination or Council of Churches.

2. The second milieu of Christian theology was the *monastic*.

Indeed, in eastern Christendom this has been its most creative environment ever since. Theology here is a function of contemplation, and its motive power is supplied by needs of the ascetic and mystical life. But, as Mr Davis notes, it has also a strong literary element. It corresponds, indeed, within the Christian Church to the movement that flowered in the wisdom literature and the scribal tradition of Judaism.

3. The third characteristic form of Christian theology was the *scholastic*, taking its distinctive colour from its university setting. Here the dominant drive has been the assimilation and communicating of learning for its own sake. This type of theology has been one of the great glories of Western Christendom. It has been the fount of pure scholarship without which the stream of theology soon becomes muddied and stagnant. Whatever the pejorative associations of the word 'academic', it is clear that no living church can afford to neglect its discipline or allow its decline.

4. Finally, in his thumbnail sketch of theological ecology Mr Davis notes since the Reformation the dominance of what he calls '*seminary* theology'. Indeed, in his own Communion post-Tridentine theology has been almost entirely shut up to the seminary, especially in a country like England. Its motive power has been the training of a professional clergy, and increasingly in all our traditions over the last hundred years the seminary has been the seed-bed (and often also the hot-house) of our theological culture. No one would deny the pervasive contribution made to the life of the Church by this tradition of teaching and study. It is the theology not of the bishop or the monk or the professor but of the pastoral counsellor,[1] and without the competence to which it has been brought in recent decades the Church would be in a sorry way. Nevertheless, 'theology in seminary confinement', as Mr Davis entitles his article, has disturbing features, especially when pursued in isolation.

But my concern is not to examine these, as he does, but to

[1] See H. Richard Niebuhr, *The Purpose of the Church and its Ministry* (Harper, New York, 1956), pp. 80-90.

TOWARDS A GENUINELY LAY THEOLOGY 63

ask whether in the twentieth century we are not being challenged to yet a fifth theological type. It is certainly not to be seen as an alternative to the other four, any more than they supersede each other. Nevertheless, if we fail to develop it and remain content with the theologies shaped by the creative forces of other situations, we may default disastrously on the task ahead of us.

For want of a better term, I will call this fifth type a *lay* theology. By that, of course, I do not mean an amateur as opposed to a professional theology. Nor do I mean a theology for the laity in the narrow sense of those who are not clergymen, though one would expect its distinctive character to be moulded by laymen, in the same way as the typical practitioners of episcopal theology have been those charged with *episcope* in the Church of God. In its essence it is a theology which is impelled by the needs of the *laos*, or whole people of God, to *be* the Church *in* the world. Just as in the past it has been the councils of the Church, the monasteries, the universities, the training seminaries, that have been the springs from which new theological thinking has been fed into the Church, so tomorrow I would expect its creative source to be the engagement of the *laos* in the life of the world.

The organs through which this theological thinking will most distinctively be done have yet to be fashioned. But the embryonic forms of them are doubtless visible in the lay institutes, the evangelical academies, the ecumenical centres, and, in much humbler but no less important ways, the listening-posts of Christian presence and Christian dialogue in a predominantly post-religious world. In Britain, with the illusion that the inherited structures are still fundamentally viable, we have been forced to less radically new thinking and action than either on the Continent of Europe or in some circles in America. In America, indeed, the traditional structures are far stronger and more successful (so much so that I recently came away feeling that at least in England we are nearer to death and so perhaps to resurrection!). But they have been subjected to searching self-scrutiny—for instance, by Peter Berger in his

Noise of Solemn Assemblies[1] and Gibson Winter in *The Suburban Captivity of the Churches*.[2] And I would draw on the latter's most recent book, *The New Creation as Metropolis*,[3] for a preliminary sketch of what such new organs of Christian ministry and theology might conceivably look like.

The concentration of the Churches on providing, or rather being, as he puts it, 'residential chaplaincies to family life,' 'preoccupied with the maintenance of emotional stability and the nurture of children', represents by now a defection amounting to apostasy; for it simply 'leaves untouched the vast structures of metropolitan life that determine the shape of our world'. In place of the medieval ideal of the Church as *the cultic organism* or the Reformation model of *the confessional assembly*, he sees *the prophetic fellowship* as the only relevant form of 'the servant Church in a secularized world'.

This, he insists, means nothing less than an institutional revolution for the Church. It means taking with absolute seriousness 'the servanthood of the laity' in the world 'not as a nice addition to round off a professional ministry but as *the* ministry of the Church'. At present all talk of the training and ministry of the laity silently assumes that the religious organization (of which the professional minister is firmly in charge) is the base and springboard of the Church's apostolate. 'Such a view of the apostolate misconceives the nature of contemporary society and the depth of the alienation of the churches from the dynamic forces of our world. The training of an apostolate has to occur where the laity find themselves engaged *in* worldly responsibilities.' 'The platform for mission' is not something constructed by the Church, but 'the organizational structure shaping this world'.

This involves a reversal of amost all of our traditional presuppositions. It requires a form of the Church, as I suggested earlier, as leaven within, rather than an institution alongside, the structures of the world. 'Thus', he says, 'the evangelical

[1] Doubleday, New York, 1961.
[2] Doubleday, New York, and SCM Press, London, 1961.
[3] Macmillan, New York and London, 1963.

TOWARDS A GENUINELY LAY THEOLOGY 65

centres and academies will not be auxiliaries to the residential churches; they will be the Church in the new society'. The roles of clergy and laity are transposed: 'The ministry is usually conceived today as the work of clergymen with auxiliary aids among the laity; ministry in the servant Church is the work of laity in the world with auxiliary help from theological specialists.'

An example of this is the change that comes over the ministry of *proclamation*. In the confessional, congregational pattern of church life to which we are used this means *preaching* by the clergy *to* a passive and docile laity. In the prophetic fellowship 'preaching in the worldly structures, where it occurs, would be a layman's task. The clergyman is primarily needed as a theological resource for this lay apostolate.' But in fact proclamation is not to be identified with preaching: it primarily takes the form of what, perhaps not altogether happily, he calls 'theological reflection'. This means discerning in depth, and disclosing in inter-personal commitment, the true meaning 'in Christ' of the history which secular man has the terrible and ineluctable responsibility of shaping. 'The Church as prophetic fellowship has no escape hatches from this history into a superhistory; she is only open to the same history and more committed to shape the same future for which she knows herself responsible.' Like Jeremiah purchasing a piece of land in the ravaged country, she witnesses to the prophetic future of metropolis as the New Mankind. 'Hence, engagement in the world, responsibility for shaping that world, becomes the milieu of proclamation, and ultimately the proper milieu of confession and worship.'

The relation to all this of loyalty to the institutional churches and their religious obligations becomes acutely problematic. 'One begins to ask what, if anything, the Church has to do with the case. Why are men not simply called to be human in their historical obligations, for this is man's true end and his salvation?' But the servant Church must reclaim for a secularized world the preaching and sacramental life which have been confined to the religious glass-case by the confessional and cultic forms of the Church. 'We have frozen the cultic moment in the congregational assembly. When the cultic life of the servant Church becomes integral to the ministry of the laity, we shall see celebration of the Lord's Supper in the contexts of our communal life.' Similarly, 'preaching will have to become more integral to the tasks of apostolate and pastorate' (both seen primarily as *lay* activities). The trouble is that 'the confessional assembly . . . provides an impoverished setting for preaching'. 'In the prophetic fellowship, much of this work will have to be carried on through group processes of biblical reflection.' Only so, and with the trained help of clergy released from the consuming demands of the religious organization, is there a hope of meeting the requirement of 'secular Christianity' that 'the laity, who represent the secular, become theologically far more astute than at any other period in Christian history'.

I have spelt out these ideas because I think they point in the right direction, not because I necessarily follow them all the way (I question, as I imagine, if pressed, he would, his simple identification of 'the Church' with 'the evangelical centres and academies', which are after all no more than aids—and problematic ones at that). At the moment, the matrices of a distinctively lay theology are very embryonic. It is easy from within the established structures of church and university to regard these new forms, struggling to be born, as puny affairs. And it would in fact be a disastrous impoverishment if such lay theology were forced to come to fruition in isolation from the traditional centres of theological engagement, the councils of the Church,[1] the religious communities, the universities and the seminaries. For unless it is planted in these and can draw upon their resources, it will be stunted for lack of depth of earth. Nevertheless, if these bodies are to take it into their

---

[1] It is to the credit of the leadership of the World Council of Churches to have sponsored more thinking on lay theology than all the other groups put together. See, especially, *Laity* (the Bulletin of the Department of the Laity) and *Concept* (Papers from the Department on Studies in Evangelism), obtainable from the British Council of Churches, 10 Eaton Gate, London, SW1, at 3s. 6d. and 2s. 6d. per copy respectively.

systems they must expect it to disturb many of their presuppositions. For it will seem as secular *vis à vis* the theology of the seminary as the scholastic was secular *vis à vis* the monastic. And to the academic it will appear dangerously existential, just as to the episcopal it looks disconcertingly popular—by-passing not only the hard-back but often the pulpit as well.

Worldly Divinity

But let me try to describe more closely what I envisage by such a distinctively lay theology (which is *not* what hitherto we have tended to mean by theology for the laity, i.e. academic or seminary theology diluted). By it I mean a theology which *starts* from the Christian's involvement in the world *now*. It means thinking theologically about *this world*. This is its point of departure, wherever subsequently it may be led.

Now this is simply not happening at the moment in any serious or planned way. Yet there is a widespread avidity for precisely this—not, as I see it, primarily for 'religion' but for a theology that makes sense of life in the mid-twentieth century. This, as the response has shown, is the point of theological interest, but the fact remains that men and women cannot go on to *study* at the point at which their concern is engaged. There is no course for which one could enrol that would begin by taking one on from it: academic theology starts at quite a different place. Moreover, all the books that have created the ferment are essentially side-lines for the theologians concerned. They are not on the themes to which they are being compelled to devote their time, teaching or research. Certainly the only books of mine which have circulated at all widely—*On Being the Church in the World* and *Honest to God*—represent what I have been able or forced to do on the side. They are essentially amateur efforts, off my real subject. They are not, professionally speaking, what would be regarded as serious theology, of the sort that I would dare include in a submission, say, for a Doctorate of Divinity—though I reckon they probably include as much original theology as any of my academically respectable books. But the point is that for most people they represent much the most serious kind of theology—in fact the only theology they feel worth taking seriously.

I remember very much the same feeling when I myself was a student. I think I can say that I learnt more theology which has subsequently been of vital concern to me as a Christian in the world from the Student Christian Movement than I ever did from the University Faculty. I believe there is a dangerous gap here. The traditional theology purveyed by the universities is essentially prolegomena. It is the grammar of the subject and is linguistically and historically centred. However much it may be made relevant by imaginative teaching, the centre of gravity (which I suppose is somewhere between the first century and the fifth) is miles away from the centre of concern. The result, as one sees from the clergy, is that most of us who read theology as students quickly give it up as a matter of living concern. It really only equips those who subsequently wish to teach it. And consequently most of the research produced by those who do go on with it is affected by this starting-point. As Bishop E. R. Wickham has observed,[1] 'It is surprising how little of the richness and variety of modern theological writing bites on the modern world.' Who, for instance, is producing a theology of power, of matter, of secularization and socialization, which are the real things which are shaping our lives? There seems to me an urgent need that a deliberate start should be made from the other end.

Where can we do this? My answer would be at every level.[2] We must see it happening in the schools, where Religious Instruction in Britain is suffering from exactly the same malaise of irrelevance and lack of bite on any of the real

---

[1] *Church and People in an Industrial City*, p. 222; and see his most recent book, *Encounter with Modern Society*, Lutterworth Press, London, 1964.

[2] See the wide-ranging and heartening symposium on 'Theology in Education' in *Theology*, October 1964, which underscores many of the things said here.

problems that engage children and teenagers.[1] I am sure that it has got to happen in our lay training, in the dioceses and parishes. Indeed, to the credit of those pioneering it, this is the place at the moment where most is happening, though it is still pathetically little. I am certain too that it has to be taken much more seriously at the Church's colleges of theology. I use this term deliberately rather than theological colleges (which in England means what elsewhere would be called seminaries), as it should include all kinds of institutes both for laity and clergy, such, as I said earlier, we in England have still not got, despite the plea for such 'organs of thinking' in Bishop Wickham's book.[2] There is indeed, hopefully, the possibility of a new look to English theological education, for instance, in the enlarged Queen's College, Birmingham, and in the thinking focused in the Theological Education Committee of the Central Advisory Council for the Ministry. I would also draw attention to the excellent chapter on 'Training the Parson to Work with the Layman' in Mark Gibbs and Ralph Morton, *God's Frozen People*, with its potentially revolutionary statement: 'The fundamental training on which the future of the Church depends is the training of the laity and . . . the training of the clergy has to be seen as fitting into and serving this.'[3] But to my mind the most exciting possibilities of beginning theological training from the other end, of involvement—and indeed of almost total immersion—in the world, are to be seen in the projected syllabus of the Urban Training Centre for Christian Mission in Chicago.[4]

But ultimately I believe it is what happens in the universities that will be decisive.[5] This is particularly true in Britain and

---

[1] See Harold Loukes, *Teenage Religion* (SCM Press, London, 1961); Richard Acland, *We Teach Them Wrong* (Gollancz, London, 1963); Ronald Goldman, *Religious Thinking from Childhood to Adolescence* (Routledge and Kegan Paul, London, 1964); and Appendix II below.

[2] *Op. cit.*, pp. 257-61.

[3] *Op. cit.*, p. 179.

[4] Obtainable from 40 North Ashland Avenue, Chicago, Ill.

[5] A growingly important aspect of this is the section of the university which is itself 'in the world', namely, the extra-mural department. For an imaginative description of what can be done, and perhaps uniquely done,

on the Continent of Europe, where the centre of gravity of theological teaching and the weight of resources of money and manpower are still in the state-supported universities rather than in the Church's colleges. But in any case they are crucial for a genuinely lay theology. For this is where the great mass of the students already are, with the time and the money for full-time study. How can we help them, whatever their subject, to see the world they are going to serve in some depth and perspective before they are thrown into it? Can their training to think theologically take its start from *this* world, rather than from the literary sources and historical origins of Christianity?

When it comes to specific recommendations, it is impossible to prescribe any blue-print, since the undergraduate study of theology differs so greatly—and the necessary correctives may be correspondingly different. In England (especially in the ancient universities), and even more in Germany, Switzerland and Scandinavia, the only way in, at an honours level, for an interested layman is a heavily linguistic and historical course designed chiefly for specialists. In the British situation (which is the only one I can speak about from the inside) I should want to plead for the option of a 'modern' as well as a 'classical' side to the study of theology—primarily for laymen, but also as a more living introduction to the subject for many ordinands.[1] It would be a calamity if the two approaches were

---

here, especially on the frontiers of theology with architecture, the arts, sociology, psychology, medicine, etc., see the report *Theology for Adults* by Gilbert Cope, Staff Tutor in Theology at the University of Birmingham (obtainable from the Church of England Board of Education, 69 Great Peter St., London, S.W.1, price 2s 6d).

It is worth noting too that almost all the lectures of the Southwark Ordination Course (syllabus from 16 Duke St. Hill, London, S.E.1), which enables men to train for the priesthood while remaining at their work, are arranged by the Department of Extra-Mural Studies of London University.

[1] An encouraging step is the new Section VI of Part III of the Theological Tripos at Cambridge, 'Christian Theology in the Modern World' (for which I began pressing before I left the Faculty Board of Divinity in 1959). The limitation of this is that it is intended to be taken at the post-graduate stage. I am particularly concerned to see an opening for the

pursued in isolation or without cross-fertilization, and I value Richard Niebuhr's definition of a theological school as a 'centre of the Church's intellectual activity . . . in which the biblical, the historical and the contemporary Church are included in one community of discourse'.[1] But in any one *syllabus* one has to recognize the severe limitation of time available. Indeed, if necessary, I should be prepared to cut losses drastically and advocate that the 'modern' course should start quite boldly with the twentieth century—though, naturally, whenever one digs in one has to reckon with roots that go much farther back.

Simply for illustration, I would suggest such subjects as these:

1. *Twentieth-century Church History*. The live movements in this will inevitably force a study in greater depth to know what they are talking about (e.g. the trends in biblical theology, the liturgical movement, the ecumenical movement, the recovery of the laity).
2. *A Twentieth-century Theology of Mission*. This should deal with the engagement of the Christian faith on the frontiers of twentieth-century thought and society. I cannot see why a book like F. Boulard's *Introduction to Religious Sociology*[2] should not be just as possible a starting-point as an introduction to the apostolic age—and just as possible to examine. A notable example of what can be pioneered in this field has been the work of

---

regular run of honours undergraduates who having done what they require *academically* (though not necessarily professionally) for the technical, business or administrative jobs to which they will be going, would like to spend their final year, or where possible two years, not on further specialist qualifications but on trying to see things whole. What in Cambridge terms I am asking for is a 'modern' alternative in Parts Ia and II of the Theological Tripos to which a student can switch after Part I in another subject. There are heartening possibilities of integrating theology with other modern studies in some of the new universities.

[1] *Op. cit.*, p. 127.
[2] Translated by M. J. Jackson (Darton, Longman and Todd, London, 1960).

J. C. Hoekendijk as Professor of Twentieth Century Church History at Utrecht.[1]

3. *Contemporary Systematic Theology.* This I would define as the area between the philosophy of religion and dogmatics. The latter is essentially something that takes place inside the Church, whereas I think what is needed is what Tillich (its towering exponent) calls an 'answering theology', which takes place *between* the Church and the world. It is in this area that the great questions of our day are to be found, and though they may be profound and agonizing I do not think that they are the most difficult for the modern young person to get into. Indeed, I believe that he can far more instinctively feel himself inside the mind of a man like Bonhoeffer or Tillich than many of the theologians' theologians. I reckon that my theological education began when I was plunged in at the deep end with Reinhold Niebuhr (at the SCM Conference at Swanwick in 1939), and though we found him difficult, we never found him forbidding (like the *History of Israel* which finally converted me to come into academic theology through the philosophy of religion!).

4. *Contemporary Ethics.* Here again I believe that this should start not from pure principles but from present problems, and allow ethical theory (e.g. of punishment, sex, war or race) to emerge from an immersion in the actual issues of contemporary society.

To the details of what I have suggested I attach no particular weight. I do, however, believe strongly that the universities have a very special responsibility, both to Church and State, if the age into which we are being propelled is to be interpreted with any kind of theological penetration. Much lay theology is at the moment regrettably amateur stuff—and this is not the fault of those who are being left to do it. For most of the best

---

[1] See his collected articles, *De Kerk Binnenste Buiten*, Ten Have, Amsterdam, 1964. To be translated into English under the title *The Church Inside Out* and published by the Westminster Press, Philadelphia, and the SCM Press, London.

minds going out from our schools, colleges and seminaries are simply not being sensitized to its needs and problems. If our economics courses sent men out with as little awareness of applied economics as our theological courses do of applied theology, the nation would have reason to complain.

The Creative Centre

But what is at stake is the health, not only of the nation, but of theology as a living discipline. Unless it can rediscover itself, I believe it is in danger of withering away as a subject to be taken seriously in the modern world—just as scholastic theology, unless it had been renewed at the springs of the Renaissance, stood in danger of withering away with Ptolemaic astronomy. For, as Mr Howard Root says in his opening essay in *Soundings*,[1] 'academic theology has lived on its own fat. The supply of fat is running out.' I do not in the least want to see the classical disciplines of theology discredited—that would be disastrous for lay theology as much as for any other. But if we are not to retire to the ark or die of inanition, we must find new sources of nourishment. In Mr Root's words again, 'We have relied upon the several establishments, religious, political and moral, to protect us from the barbarians. Our first lesson will be to learn that our greatest ally is not the dying establishments but the hungry and destitute world which is still alive enough to feel its own hunger. The starting-point for natural theology is . . . sharpened awareness.'

And this links, finally, with another piece of writing by Charles Davis, from whom I began. It is an essay of his in a recent Downside symposium on *Theology and the University*.[2] I do not propose to quote from it except to borrow the extended passage from John Wain's autobiography, *Sprightly Running*, which serves, as it were, as his text. Mr Wain is

[1] 'Beginning All Over Again', p. 19.
[2] Ed. J. Coulson (Darton, Longman and Todd, London, 1964).

describing the work of the creative artist. Mr Davis's thesis is that what he says ought to be true, and pre-eminently true, of the creative theologian.

'To write well' means far more than choosing the apt word or the telling arrangement of syllables, though it means these things as well; it is a matter of feeling and living at the required depth, fending off the continual temptation to be glib and shallow, to appeal to the easily aroused response, to be evasive and shirk the hard issues. It is a matter of training oneself to live with reality, and, as our greatest living poet has warned us, 'Human kind cannot bear very much reality'. But, if one is to write well, one *must* bear it; increasing the dose, perhaps, until one can absorb it in quantities that would unhinge the ordinary person. This is a large claim; if what I am saying is true, the artist is better (stronger, braver, more perceptive) than the ordinary person. I shrink from my own meaning, for who can really enjoy making such a claim, with the responsibility it involves? But the claim must be made, and the responsibility shouldered, even if I myself never succeed in writing one good book.

For if the responsibility is great, and the risk of ignominious failure greater still, the reward is in proportion. An author, if he is big enough, can do so much for his fellow men. He can put words into their mouths and reasons into their heads; he can fill their sleep with dreams so potent that when they awake they will go on living them. I have said that people live according to their mental pictures. . . . And where do the mental pictures come from? There is no one simple answer, but I believe that the most powerful and widespread mental pictures, those which dominate the thought and action of a whole epoch, can usually be traced to the work of a few men, the supreme artists, the imaginative creators of their time. It does not matter that the majority get those pictures at second hand, or at tenth or fiftieth hand; they come from the centre—and are merely more blurred and simplified as they move outwards. There, at that centre, are the artists who really form the consciousness of their time; they respond deeply, intuitively, to what is happening, what has happened and what will happen, and their response is expressed in metaphor and symbol, in image and fable. To be one of that band, to inhabit that creative centre, is the ambition of every author who has not sold out.

That, I believe, should be the vocation held out to every theologian. It is a call in the first place not to relevance in any slick sense but to exposure, to compassion, sensitivity, awareness and integrity.[1] It is the call to bear reality, more reality than it is easy or indeed possible for a human being to bear unaided. It is to be with God in his world. And in each epoch or culture the place of the theologian is to stand as near as he may to the 'creative centre' of God's world in his day. And, at their best and most vigorous, that is where the various theologies I listed have been found. Episcopal theology has been done (and still has to be done) at the point where 'the establishment' shapes the forces of society—in the councils of princes or their equivalents in Church and State. Monastic theology was vital and creative for its age because it flowed from the centres of conservation and renewal within the world of its day—and the theological contribution, for example, of the Iona Community in Scotland, or the Petits Frères and the Taizè Community in France, or the Zöe Brotherhood in Greece, shows that this is no spent need. Scholastic theology was able to mould the body and soul of Western society—and win its place as queen of the sciences—because it stood at the fountain-head of that society's culture, the medieval university; and no one need argue today for the vital role of a genuinely integrated theological faculty in a modern university. Even seminary theology, though it may appear to have flourished somewhat more in the enclaves of society, has exercised its widespread influence because it has been an organic part of the general professionalization of life in capitalist and managerial society. To take an example from the United States, where seminary theology is to be seen at its most impressive,

[1] On the function of the artist in society, see also the striking quotations in Martin Jarrett-Kerr, *The Secular Promise* (SCM Press, London, 1964, and Fortress Press, Philadelphia), pp. 148-50, and in Colin W. Williams, *Where in the World?*, pp. 95-6. Both could, and should, apply *mutatis mutandis* to the theologian. For the point where the creative artist and theologian meet, see Arthur C. McGill, *The Celebration of Flesh: Poetry in Christian Life* (Association Press, New York, 1964, and Peter Smith, Derby, 1965) and K. M. Baxter, *Speak What We Feel: A Christian Looks at the Contemporary Theatre* (SCM Press, London, 1964).

the Harvard Divinity School has owed its influence upon the American way of life to the extent that it has been part of the same creative movement which produced the Harvard Business School and the Harvard Medical School and the Harvard Law School.

My plea is that theologians should take stock of where they stand in relation to the 'creative centre' of the age into which we are moving and of the 'coming great Church' which one trusts will be there to baptize it. There are plentiful signs that theology need not be a dead discipline: in fact, it is probably more 'on the map' in Britain today than it has been for a hundred years. And yet it remains true that for the ordinary person—and indeed for most practical purposes for the ordinary parson—theology as it is generally understood and purveyed is miles away (and probably getting further) from the creative centres of our new society. Indeed, Mr Harold Wilson, who would doubtless like to see himself as the embodiment of that new society, accurately reflected the current 'image' of theology, when, in his dispute with Hugh Gaitskell over the famous Clause Four of the Labour Party constitution (on nationalization), he sought to dismiss the whole thing as 'theology'—theoretical discussion bearing no vital relation to the real concerns that made the Party 'tick'. Increasingly, to men of the second industrial revolution, theology seems to belong, if not to the 'grouse moors', at any rate to the small shopkeepers, of the spiritual world. And both its retailers and wholesalers have sheltered for too long behind a Retail Price Maintenance which is fast breaking down.

'Where', asks Howard Root,[1] 'do we look now for faithful, stimulating, profound accounts of what it is to be alive in the twentieth century? The inevitable answer to that question carries a judgment. We look to the poet or novelist or dramatist or film producer. In creative works of art we see ourselves better and come into touch with just those sources of imagination which should nourish efforts in natural theology. . . . This is only another way of saying that theologians cannot direct

[1] *Op. cit.*, p. 18.

men's minds to God until they are themselves steeped in God's world and in the imaginative productions of his most sensitive and articulate creatures.' And as long as that description includes the work of scientists and technicians, philosophers and even politicians, it may stand as a sufficient summary of my plea for a deliberate shift in the bias of our studies towards a genuinely lay theology. Without such a shift any new Reformation will rapidly wither away.

4

LIVING IN THE OVERLAP

'WE are those upon whom the ends of the ages have met (or overlapped).'[1] Whatever St Paul may have meant by that in its original context, it may stand for the fact that *we* are called to live in the overlap between two ages. Just as there was a period in which the medieval and Renaissance worlds existed side by side and men found themselves living in different degrees or with different parts of themselves in both at once, so today we are committed, at any rate for our life-time, to this bewildering double existence. In the case of the previous Reformation the hangover from the Middle Ages lasted for many centuries: indeed, in many Latin countries, and in large areas of the conscious and unconscious life of each one of us, it has not ended yet. This time the transition is bound to be more rapid and more radical—and all the more disconcerting while it lasts. In the process we shall be split down the middle, and the tensions within the Church between old and new will stretch it to breaking-point. But if it is not to shiver in the process, as it did last time, it is essential that we work from both ends at once, starting from within the traditional presuppositions and from outside them, and that each side recognizes and respects the operations of the other.

I spoke in my second chapter of the need to begin at the other end—and, indeed, I shall continue to emphasize this approach, since the vast weight of the Church's resources is at present committed at the traditional end of the bridge. Nevertheless, unless we are to have an even more disastrous schism than last time, it is imperative that we do reform from both ends. For if one thing is certain, it is that the past will go on

[1] I Corinthians 10.11.

into the future with all its accumulated momentum—just as the medieval churches are still with us, in original or reproduction, and indeed continue to dominate our landscapes. And unless the change begins from inside the old as well as outside it, then the old will not only grow more and more moribund but will drive the radicals to schism and frustration in the wilderness. And nothing could be further from anything that I desire.

For I believe strongly that the true radical is and must be a man of roots. In words that I have used elsewhere,[1] 'The revolutionary can be an "outsider" to the structure he would see collapse: indeed, he must set himself outside it. But the radical goes to the roots of his *own* tradition. He must love it: he must weep over Jersualem, even if he has to pronounce its doom.' Any re-formation must start from within, and in the case of the Church must respect the fact that the life it would see renewed is the organic life of a Body deeply rooted in the processes of history. It is not only, I think, because I am an Englishman that I see reformation marked as much by evolution as by revolution. To be realistic we must begin where we are—with the plant, the liturgy, the ministry, the money and the organization we have got. We must be prepared to involve ourselves in the burden and struggle of seeing that it is less irrelevant, less wasteful, less sheerly frustrating than it is. Nothing is gained by simply cutting oneself off from the main body and getting out on a limb. Indeed, it is essential to have the humility to see oneself as part of the sin and irrelevance that has to be overcome—from within.

One must start from inside the tradition one has inherited—for no reformation comes as a clean break. And yet I am convinced that one has to start from the other end at the same time. And here the situation is different from that of sixteenth-century Europe. Then one could assume, rightly or wrongly, that everyone was within the tradition, a part of the *Corpus Christianum*. (The only reference to the missionary task of the

[1] 'On Being a Radical', *The Listener*, 21 February 1963, reproduced in part in *The Honest to God Debate*, pp. 27-9.

Church in the 1662 *Book of Common Prayer* is to 'the natives on our plantations'!) But today that assumption is palpably false—and no modification or recasting of the tradition will in itself affect those who stand outside it. Indeed, with a large part of one's being one lives outside it oneself. For if one is a man of one's times one has one foot in a world to which the traditional Christian categories are increasingly alien. One has to live in this overlap emotionally and spiritually. And the strain of it can be very exhausting. The temptation of the churchman (as I know only too well) is to live in only one world—to remain within the tradition and to operate as best one can from that end by bringing it up to date and titivating the orthodoxy, or, alternatively, to abandon hope of doing anything from inside the organized Church structure altogether. It is, I am convinced, a temptation that must be resisted with one's whole being.

Let me try to illustrate what acceptance of this 'double life' means for the churchman of the new Reformation. And I do not disguise the fact that it is a most confusing and, in the proper sense of the word, distracting situation. Almost anything would be more comfortable.

1. *In Doctrine*

First I would speak briefly (since I have already touched on it) about the position in doctrine. I said in the preface to *Honest to God* that the gulf must probably grow wider before it is bridged between those who start from the end of revitalizing the traditional formulations and those who know that the attempt must also be made to begin again from a different end altogether. I doubt indeed if the gulf is likely to be bridged in our generation at all. We are in for a period when there will be no agreed synthesis as to 'what the Church teaches', and it will be easy for those within the traditional camp to shout 'Heresy!' We shall have to live with theological explorations that do not come to rest neatly in the classic formulations. And many of them will be tentative and inadequate. But I am equally sure that recastings of the traditional formulae, however dogmatically orthodox, will also be inadequate—simply because they come from this end.

Let me illustrate this from a humble example within the life of the Church—the Catechism. The Reformation, and subsequently the Counter-Reformation, brought a flood not only of new confessions but of new catechisms. Now the presupposition of a catechism is instruction given by a teaching Church which knows the answers to questions it itself asks. And no one would deny that there is still a place and a hunger for instruction. It is what we are told (usually by the clergy) that the laity constantly want more of—and I partly believe it. In any case it is the job of the teaching Church to make its instruction as fresh and intelligent as it can. And so the Church of England has recently issued a *Revised Catechism*.[1] And a very serviceable piece of work it is. Despite the fact that the backwoodsmen in Convocation insisted on restoring the Devil (thus replacing a less mythological description of evil for the young), it is an excellent piece of restatement. I am all for having a twentieth-century rather than a sixteenth-century exposition of the Faith to place in people's hands.

But I suspect in fact that it will be increasingly unused. I doubt if the new Reformation will produce any catechisms, for the whole assumption on which they rest is being undermined. It is not the Church that puts *its* question and waits to hear *its* answers returned to it. It is the world that puts the questions—and refuses to accept any prefabricated answers. The only authority it acknowledges is that which authenticates itself as such in the search for truth. 'A church which thinks that it can go on dictating truths rather than sitting with the people and working out the real questions is certainly not living in solidarity with men today.' Those last words come from the lecture I quoted earlier by Albert van den Heuvel on 'The Humiliation of the Church'.[2] He went on:

> I am not suggesting that there are no truths, or that the Church

[1] SPCK, London, 1962.　　　　　[2] See p. 14.

does not know them. I only suggest that modern people do not understand given truths. . . . Therefore religious instruction cannot be given with a simple catechism book any longer. The question and answer period has to be replaced by the question after question period, in which the answer may be found, the question may disappear, or the questions may stand unanswered. Until now the authority concept of most of our churches has been imposed. We talk because we know. And we hardly know how painful this is to those who listen to us.

Our theology has to be done from both ends at once—and there is no guarantee that the lines will meet. We simply have to trust the truth we serve, knowing that for our Master too it led to a cross, on which the gulf between God and man *appeared* at that moment wider than ever.

2. *In Liturgy*

Just as our doctrine can no longer be expounded simply from one end as what 'the Bible says' or 'the Church teaches', so in the sphere of liturgy we have a new and more complex situation on our hands.

The previous Reformation produced a great liturgical ferment and many new patterns of worship. But all of them, except those of the Quakers and the left-wing sects, started from the presuppositions of the old. Indeed, we are now seeing how so many of the basic assumptions of the Reformers about liturgy were simply carried over, in new dress, from the later Middle Ages. In particular, the fundamental clericalization of the liturgy was only very superficially affected by the transition from old priest to new presbyter.

Our generation is also in the throes of an exciting liturgical ferment. There is every indication that it will be more radical than anything that took place at the Reformation. I am one of those who feel the urgency and centrality of liturgical renewal and am convinced that we must do everything we can to make the traditional forms meaningful and relevant. I have in fact written on this subject in *Liturgy Coming to Life*,[1] and I do not, I hope, need to produce further evidence that I believe that beginning from this end is vitally important. Indeed, the importance of it was vividly brought home to me at the week-end group I mentioned earlier, where, somewhat to my surprise, a high-light of the week-end proved to be the Sunday service to which I was previously committed—a celebration of Baptism, Confirmation and Communion restored, as in the early Church, to a single liturgical whole. It showed that the traditional liturgy of the Church well and imaginatively done still has power to provide hooks for people's eyes—and it is just as important to start from the hooks as from the eyes.

Nevertheless, I am increasingly convinced that the Liturgical Movement, however revivifying, is not of itself going to meet the demands of the new Reformation. One has to start from right out the other end as well, with those for whom the whole notion of organized religion and services in church, and indeed worship itself as usually understood, provides absolutely no way in at all. When one sees at first hand the utter irrelevance—and indeed positive deterrent—which the whole idea of 'going to church' presents to many of our generation in their search for a meaningful theology of life, one can only be appalled that 99 per cent of the Church's money, time and ministry appears to be geared to the object of getting them there. If liturgy is to come to life for them, no amount of revising our services will make the difference. It is a question of starting not from liturgy but from life, and helping them to see (*if we can ourselves see it*) that liturgy is primarily a secular rather than a religious activity. 'The roots of the liturgy', to take the title of Eric James's admirable pamphlet[2] on that theme, are in society rather than in church. As I seek to bring out in my own book, it has to do with social action, with the use of matter, with life in community—with how, in fact, the common

---

[1] Mowbray, London, 1960 and 1963 (with a new preface); Westminster Press, Philadelphia, 1964.
[2] *Prism* Pamphlet, No. 1, 1962 (obtainable from Blue Star House, London, N.19, price 1*s* 6*d*).

can be made holy. The trouble is that it has lost its living roots in the soil of the world and become a pot-plant in the sanctuary of the Church. Even for most church people, I doubt if the scales can fall from their eyes until they see it growing naturally again—out of the ordinary sharing of ordinary life, as in the cottage at Emmaus.

As a very modest illustration of what starting from life rather than liturgy might mean, I would tentatively mention some exploration we have been doing at our own family table.

Despite the fact that our children have been at Parish Communion almost every Sunday of their lives from the carry-cot onwards, it was becoming increasingly clear that most of it simply passed them by, because the service in church corresponded with nothing concrete in their everyday experience and relationships. A dissatisfaction with family prayers, with Communion preparation, with grace before meals—together with the fact that I was so frequently out when the children were home—combined to make us resolve to set aside one meal in the week (at present supper on Saturday), to which we would all give a priority and which we would make a sort of family celebration. It is not a Eucharist, but a rather special meal, to which we all look forward, which includes a bottle of wine.[1] The procedure is extremely flexible, but at the moment we normally begin (in winter) by lighting the table candles and singing the very early Christian hymn, 'Hail, gladdening Light'.[2] Then in prayer we share freely whatever is concerning us, our doings and our relations, bringing in also those with whom we shall be meeting at the Lord's Table the next morning. At the close of this we say together an adapted verse of a eucharistic hymn:[3]

> Come, risen Lord, and deign to be our guest;
> Nay, let us be thy guests; the feast is thine;
> Thyself at thine own board make manifest,
> In this our fellowship of bread and wine.

[1] In Lent we have soup and water, and make it a war-on-want supper.
[2] In John Keble's fine version, *Hymns Ancient and Modern*, No. 18.
[3] By G. W. Briggs (*Songs of Praise*, No. 266).

I then cut a slice from the loaf and pour out a glass of wine, both of which we pass round, ending with a salutation, or the grace, and a joining of hands. After the meal we do some Bible study based on the Epistle or the Gospel for the next day, and end the evening by playing a family game.

It was not till after we had worked this out from our own needs that I discovered that our 'rite' corresponded with fascinating closeness to an early form of the Agape in the Eastern church, recorded in some versions of Hippolytus' *Apostolic Tradition*.[1] This seems to me a paradigm of how liturgy should grow: not from antiquarian precedents, but from life—enriched by the overtones of the centuries.[2]

I am sure it is at the house-church level that we are most likely to discover or rediscover what we want to do in liturgy. But we must go on to relate this to our gatherings in larger (but still face-to-face) groups. As lively illustrations, I would instance the accounts[3] by George W. Webber of 'Worship in East Harlem'[4] and Horst Symanowski, 'Sunday in an Industrial Mission'.[5]

What we do at the parish level still leaves endless room for exploration—and for tension between tradition and experiment. What can be achieved by a radical break-away is excitingly illustrated in the story[6] of the Church of the Saviour,

[1] Quoted in full by Gregory Dix, *The Shape of the Liturgy* (Dacre Press, London, 1945), pp. 85-6.

[2] Since I have not followed up here what I said in *Honest to God* about the way private prayer must also start from life, I should like simply to commend, as a most striking example of this, the book by the French priest Michel Quoist, *Prayers of Life* (English translation, Gill, Dublin, 1963).

[3] In the World Council of Churches' bulletin *Concept*, No. 1, March 1962. Here again much of the most radical new thinking is being channelled through the WCC, which has a study-group on public worship chaired by J. C. Hoekendijk and J. G. Davies.

[4] See also his *God's Colony in Man's World* and *The Congregation in Mission* (Abingdon Press, New York, 1960 and 1964) and Bruce Kenrick, *Come Out the Wilderness* (Harper and Row, New York, and Collins, London, 1963).

[5] See also his book quoted earlier, *The Christian Witness in Industrial Society*.

[6] Elizabeth O'Connor, *Call to Commitment* (Harper and Row, New York, 1963).

Washington, D.C., whose headquarters is simply a large Victorian house. Most of us, of course, have to start with the ecclesiastical buildings we have got, and the adaptation of them is a high priority.[1] But I confess that when I see the budgets expended on the maintenance, heating and staffing of our innumerable churches I want to ask St Paul's question to the Corinthians: 'Have you no homes of your own to eat and drink in?'[2] I agree we must have public places (though not necessarily religious ones) for when the people of God 'come together to one place'. But the problem of living and planning responsibly in the overlap when it comes to decisions on church architecture, which is one of my keenest concerns, is extremely baffling. One has to start from both ends, but where one comes down in the middle it is very difficult to be sure.

But liturgy involves the consecration not only of space but of time, and this also raises perplexing problems for those upon whom 'the ends of the ages have met'. During the period of Christendom the Church imposed *its* calendar on society, and in particular it created on Sunday (what the Television Act in Britain still legalizes for seventy minutes of it) a 'religious slot', in which the Church had it to itself. It was not always thus—nor is it likely to be so much longer. One of the great achievements of the Church's calendar was what Dom Gregory Dix called 'the sanctification of time'.[3] But the danger is that what was previously the consecration of the common will simply survive as the celebration of the strange—and the Church will find itself living in a separated holy time (as in a separated holy space) while the world goes its own way. It will become a 'peculiar people', precisely in the sense which the Bible does not intend and which the author of the Epistle to Diognetus was at pains to deny when he wrote the famous words:[4] 'Christians are not distinguished from the rest of man-

---

[1] See my preface to *Making the Building Serve the Liturgy* (ed. Gilbert Cope, Mowbray, London, 1962).
[2] I Corinthians 11.22.
[3] *Op. cit.*, ch. XI.
[4] Epistle to Diognetus, 5 and 6. Trans. J. B. Lightfoot, *The Apostolic Fathers* (Macmillan, London, 1891), pp. 503-5.

kind either in locality or in speech or in customs. For they dwell not somewhere in cities of their own, neither do they use some different language, nor practise an extraordinary kind of life.' Rather, he said, 'they dwell in cities of Greeks and barbarians as the lot of each is cast, and follow the native customs in dress and food and the other arrangements of life'—and yet *within these* they exhibit a citizenship and style of life which is transformed and transforming.

For what is likely to look in retrospect a quite exceptional period in one limited geographical area the Church avoided the form of the slave by imposing its calendar on the world. To quote Albert van den Heuvel again,

> Festivals had to be observed, the Sabbath had to be celebrated, and church bells told people when to pray their morning and evening prayers at the same hours as the monks got up and went to bed. Of course urbanization and mobility, shift work and all the changes of our world have done away with a lot of these things, because they simply do not work any more. First of all, the morning and evening prayers. We indeed left them to the monks. When the calendar of the world changed from a 6-day working week to a 5-day working week, the world lost Sunday as the indication of the rhythm by which it lives. We have a week-end, and people use it very differently. For a large portion it means the space in which the mobility of society can be celebrated. More and more people will find recreational possibilities which take them away for the whole week-end. . . . The question is: what will the churches do? Will they keep imposing their Sunday and its observance on the new society, or will they study seriously what a new society asks of them and act accordingly? Would the Christian Church really suffer from—for instance—ten Christ days in the year and a few week-ends, which could take the place of the Sunday observance as we now see it disappear more and more around us?

My answer again would be that we must start from both ends. I believe the church of the new Reformation like the early Church will still observe its 'secret discipline' centred on the first day of the week and the breaking of bread. But from the other end I believe that we must be prepared to reconsider radically when and where and how we should ask people to meet. Three week-ends away together for uninterrupted growth in the common life may do more for the building up of the Body of Christ than fifty isolated hours spent in a pew really *meeting* no one. In between, the shaping of God's worth (which is the essential meaning of worship) may take place in much more secular and much more scattered units. If so, the plant we shall need is likely to be very different in function, size and location.

3. *In the Structure of the Church*

And this brings us finally to the organization and ministry of the Church, on which one could easily spend an entire chapter.

There is already a good deal of very hard thinking going on in the Church on this subject, mainly on an ecumenical basis, which has not yet reached the local parishes or even the denominational hierarchies. It is focused in the long-range study commissioned by the Third Assembly of the World Council of Churches at New Delhi in December 1961 on 'The Missionary Structure of the Congregation'. The material as it becomes available is published in *Concept* and the issues are brilliantly summarized in popular form, with many examples, in Colin W. Williams' study-book *Where in the World?*[1]

The central question raised is whether there may not be *heretical structures* in the life of the Church which do as much as—if not more than—any conceptual heresies to distort its message and frustrate its mission. I believe that anyone reflecting on the question must agree that there are. And here it is the most 'orthodox' who are the most guilty. The issue, in fact, has been forcibly raised whether the *norm* of our whole church life for a thousand years—namely, the territorial parish with its residential minister—is not itself now so restrictive of the

[1] 1963. It is obtainable from the Publications Office of the National Council of the Churches of Christ in the USA, 475 Riverside Drive, New York 27, N.Y. together with his subsequent *What in the World?* (1964). Both are to be published by the Epworth Press, London, in 1965.

Church's mission as to be the most questionable rather than the least questioned form of its presence. 'The one structure', Professor Hoekendijk has said,[1] 'which is most in need of an "ecclesiological accreditation" is . . . not the little congregation [the experimental sub-parochial or para-parochial group], but the congregation as such.'

I am not, indeed, convinced that a new Reformation would see the supersession of the local congregation as the most characteristic form of the Church's life. After all, the proportions to be reversed are so colossal. Well over 90 per cent of the clergymen of the Church of England are in the parish ministry (and the figure would be higher for the Methodists and most other denominations). Moreover, in terms of real estate and finance the Church's capital commitment to this particular form of organization is overwhelming. Nevertheless, it is relatively modern, and there have been other quite different patterns in the course of Christian history.[2]

In the first three centuries the Church had no buildings, and gathered wherever the structures of the world gave them opportunity. The missionaries followed the trade routes, meeting men and women where they found them. As people became Christians they gathered in the homes of believers or vocational groups or, if necessary, in catacombs. In the fourth century, the Church responded to the opportunities of establishment by building a limited number of large basilicas. But these were not really local churches. They were put up at the cross-roads of life, at what we should now call the 'power-centres' of culture. From them itinerant clergy radiated out, meeting men in homes, army camps, or in new and previously pagan areas. It was not till the eighth to the tenth centuries that the parish system became established, though even then a large part of

---

[1] *Concept* VII (May 1964), p. 6.
[2] See T. R. Morton, *The Household of Faith: An Essay on the Changing Pattern of the Church's Life* (Iona Community, Glasgow, 1951: USA title, *The Community of Faith*, Association Press, New York, 1954); also Colin W. Williams, 'Evangelism and the Congregation', *The Ecumenical Review*, January 1964, pp. 146-52, whose thumbnail sketch I have summarized in the following paragraph.

the Church's contact with the world was through the non-parochial work of the monasteries. Only with the Reformation was the pastoral and evangelistic mission of the Church confined to the residential congregation. The Reformers, here as elsewhere, entrenched the medieval pattern without serious structural alteration, whatever their changes in church *order*.

The familiar modern version, of a congregation composed of a cluster of organizations, is no older than Queen Victoria. There is nothing changeless about it, and it reflects in fact a basically stable society where people still lived and worked in the same place. But today people do not 'live where they live'. Increasingly, they only sleep where they live. Indeed, Hoekendijk goes so far as to say that, so far from the residential congregation being the 'one and basic type' of church structure 'which we might reform or complement but are not willing to give up altogether', 'many of our contemporaries and perhaps we ourselves have given up the congregation type already. . . . All the basic presuppositions of congregational life are foreign to our lives. And those who feel this way can only join congregational life if they are willing to live inauthentically.'[1] I believe that is an exaggeration; but it would come as so strange and shocking to many in the churches, and as so obviously true to many outside them, that it is worth underlining. We can all think of dozens of people who, if they wanted to identify themselves with some Christian concern or do something worth-while with their lives, would regard joining a local congregation or working through it as about the least relevant step to take. And this is not necessarily because their commitment to Christ is in doubt (it applies to many ordinands and clergy), but because the congregation appears to be a structure so unrelated to the real centres of men's lives and to the places where decisions are taken.

I have put this forcibly because I believe that there is also a very great deal to be said on the other side. Here as everywhere else we must begin from both ends. I am convinced we must do all we can to revivify rather than kill the parish units, and

[1] *Concept* VI, pp. 5-6.

I have for years been on the councils of *Parish and People*, whose concern is precisely this.[1] No one steeped in the whole series of parish renewal books of different communions[2] could possibly write off the congregation as an instrument of the Kingdom when it is outward-looking and takes the trouble to be sociologically relevant.

But it is unfair to expect the local worshipping community to be adequate to tasks for which it was never designed. Besides pressing on with the renewal of our existing units, it is urgently necessary that far more resources be put in at the other end (if necessary by a ruthless pruning of dead wood— and new growth—in ecclesiastical plant). And this is where I would expect to see the *distinctive* thrust of the new Reformation.

Indeed, I would not expect the characteristic movement of this Reformation to start, as it did last time, from recasting the existing structures of the Church, so that they can 'purely' reflect the Word of God and the Sacraments can be 'duly' administered (though this will be added if the Church really seeks the Kingdom of God with all it has). Rather, the movement of re-formation will come, in Colin Williams's words,[3] by the Church 'allowing *the forms* of her renewed life to grow around *the shapes of worldly need*'—provided, I would add, that 'need' is understood to cover the world in its strength as well as the world in its weakness. This may be put another way by saying[4] that our traditional habit has been to think in the order God—Church—World. But the biblical witness should have taught us differently:

---

[1] Its new journal, *Renewal News*, is obtainable from 177 Half Moon Lane, London, S.E.24, price 10s per annum.

[2] E.g. G. Michonneau, *Revolution in a City Parish* (English translation, Blackfriars, London, 1949); J. de Blank, *The Parish in Action* (Mowbray, London, 1954); T. Allan, *The Face of My Parish* (SCM Press, London, 1954); E. W. Southcott, *The Parish Comes Alive* (Mowbray, London, 1956); M. Hocking, *The Parish Seeks the Way* (Mowbray, London, 1960); T. Beeson, *New Area Mission* (Mowbray, London, 1963); R. A. Raines, *New Life in the Church* and *Reshaping the Christian Life* (Harper and Row, New York, 1961 and 1964).

[3] *Where in the World?*, p. 59.

[4] As has been stressed in the WCC discussions, particularly by Professor Georges Casalis of Paris.

God is not concerned first with the Church; and we should not think of the Church as God's sole partner, with God and the Church directing their action at the world. . . . The Church is simply part of the world—the part which is aware of Christ's Lordship over the world, and so is ready to recognize what God is doing in the world and to join him in that action.[1]

Once again, the house of God is not the Church but the world. The Church is the servant, and the first characteristic of a servant is that he lives in someone else's house, not his own. Paradoxically, the Church is also the son, the one who has the freedom of the house.[2] But Christians only too often have celebrated this freedom, as soon as they have had the chance, by setting up on their own.

What happens if we really take seriously the fact that the world must be allowed to 'write the agenda' (not the minutes!), and that the Church must take shape round the needs of the world? Obviously there are a great many needs already being met by the traditional residential congregation, and where it is functioning no one wishes to inhibit it. But to expect it to meet every need is merely to add to the frustration of those engaged in it.

For many purposes it is an instrument, not only of the wrong shape, but of the wrong size. It is both too big and too small. Admittedly, it is not a usual complaint that our congregations are too big. But most churchmen have had virtually no experience of a genuinely 'face to face' congregation—and emptying pews does not create it (rather the opposite). To be sure, this experience is being discovered in cells and house-churches, and everything must be done to press on from this end. But what is perhaps most urgently needed is not merely groups that begin from the splitting up of existing church-based congregations, but clusters that take their start and their shape from areas of the world's concern which may not have

---

[1] Colin Williams's summary, *op. cit.*, p. 76. Harvey Cox, *op. cit.*, ch. VI, 'The Church as God's Avant-garde', is a notable example of the application of this order.
[2] John 12.35-6.

anything distinctively religious about them. These 'little churches' will characteristically form around laymen or priest-workmen, who, *in their own thinking as well as in their environment*, may be as far 'out' beyond the lines of the manifest church, with its traditional categories of doctrine and worship, as the paratrooper is from the official front. They will need special understanding and support. But in the period of the 'overlap' the failures of communication are likely to be severe, with plentiful temptation to distrust on both sides. This, however, must be accepted as the price of relevance.

On the other hand, for increasingly many purposes today the congregation is too small and too local. It makes very limited sense in relating the Gospel to the principalities and powers of the modern world or indeed to the individual in the functional diversity of his public and private life. To expect the congregation to be adequate to this is simply again to deepen its sense of impotence. And yet, the congregation-centred councils and assemblies of the Church constantly suspect the growth of specialist central agencies, whose work they expect ultimately to pay off in terms of strengthening the local congregation. *But this can never be the principle of justification*, except on the assumption of the 'structural fundamentalists' that the congregation *is* the Church.

One could, of course, explore indefinitely the areas of the world's need and the consequent shape of the Church in an age of rapid social change. Simply as an indication of possible formations, the following tentative list has emerged from the working groups of the World Council of Churches[1]:

1. *Direct sociological structures* giving rise to continuing institutions—such as political structures, businesses, vocational groups, communications and entertainment media, educational and health institutions.
2. *Communities of concern* (e.g. the 'world' of the arts) and *communities of need* (e.g. drug addicts). Unlike the first group these are not so much organized institutions as

[1] Colin Williams, *op. cit.*, p. 84.

changing communities gathering around the concerns and needs.
3. *Major social crises* necessitating structural responses—e.g. race, housing, poverty, war.[1]

Naturally, the Church is already at work in most of these fields, but its structures are frequently amateurish, starved of resources, or sadly cut across by antiquated church boundaries.[2] Or it creates—or more often inherits—specifically ecclesiastical institutions, paralleling rather than permeating the structures of the world. Frequently these are hang-overs from the day when the Church pioneered services where the community at large was failing to provide them.[3] This is notably the case in regard to education in England, where there were no public authority schools till less than a century ago. But I cannot believe that, except in a few cases which could serve as laboratories for fresh experiment, the continuing Christian concern for education is now most meaningfully (let alone economically) expressed by retention of the dual system of church and state schools and training colleges.[4] If a tenth of the money was spent on intensive work with Christian and non-Christian teachers in secular schools and colleges, I believe the Church

[1] *Concept* VII (May 1964) contains a most instructive analysis of the structures thrown up by the Freedom Movement in the South of the USA, 1960-1963. A notable example of a built-in response to continuing social needs is the Friends' Committee on National Legislation in Washington, where a permanent registered lobby is maintained.

[2] For instance, quite apart from chaotically overlapping spheres of *denominational* command, the diocesan and deanery map of the Church of England finds it seriously unprepared to relate creatively and quickly to the new centres of power and responsibility in Greater London. It is a matter of ecumenical urgency that all the churches should adapt their divisions to the new boroughs rather than simply to their own pastoral and administrative conveniences.

[3] One of the things that shocks an Englishman about America is the extent to which this is still necessary in the field of social welfare.

[4] The budget of the Church Assembly has been crippled for years to come by the *second* new Church Training College at Lancaster, which I suspect will have settled down just about in time to be taken over by the State (if for no other reason because of expansion demands which the Church cannot, or should not, afford). See the devastating comments by Harvey Cox on the churches' successive roles in college education (*op. cit.*, ch. X, 'The Church and the Secular University').

might get somewhere. At the moment we are simply trying to hold back the tide of secularization at colossal and mounting expense.[1]

Indeed, I believe we should be pressing in exactly the *opposite* direction. Harvey Cox points out that one of the most important functions being performed by Christians in Eastern Europe today is assisting in the growing 'secularization' or 'de-ideologizing' of Communism. By accepting it as a political and economic system while refusing it as a religion, they are doing what the early Christians did in declining to burn incense to the Emperor while living as loyal citizens of Rome. In the same way, it could be argued that the function of the Church in Western education in the time of the new Reformation is to contribute to the secularization of secular*ism* and human*ism* as ideologies competing for the control of men's minds. And the best way to do this is not to fight a rearguard action for 'religious', let alone denominational, education, but to work for a genuinely secular (as opposed to a secularist) state, such as Christians have welcomed in India. Indeed, Michael Novak, the Roman Catholic, in his vision of 'an open Church in an open society'[2] and plea that the Church should deliberately 'make her own the forms of secular, pluralistic society', goes so far as to say:

> In the open society of our century ... the Church can live under conditions highly favourable to her inner necessities. No previous form of life was so well adapted to manifesting the message of the Gospels: the freedom of the act of faith, the free community of believers, the service of believers to their neighbors.[3]

Of course, once again in the historic situation in which we find ourselves we do not and we cannot start from scratch.

---

[1] In a recently projected diocesan capital appeal for £1 million, no less than £600,000 was for church schools. In the United States, of course, where there is no religion in state schools, the situation is entirely different. There the extravagance is in church class-room blocks (bigger than many English day-schools) which are used for *one hour a week*.

[2] A more creative formula than the old Protestant slogan of a 'free (i.e. disestablished) church in a free state'.

[3] *Op. cit.*, pp. 359-62.

In all these questions of church strategy I am convinced that we have to begin at both ends—and be prepared for the tension of it. As a bishop, I am immersed up to the hilt in the organization of the Church, and I am made aware how much of it prevents rather than enables the work of the Kingdom. I have no doubt that the machinery of the Church of England is more antiquated and rusty than most, and it would be easy to produce scarifying stories of the devious means one has to use to get from A to B. But the difference between our various religious establishments is only one of degree. The organization Church has an immense built-in inertia and I am sure it is utterly unrealistic to think that one can by-pass the tedious, time-consuming process of reshaping it. That is why, with qualifications, I support, and indeed have been closely involved with, the Paul Report on *The Deployment and Payment of the Clergy*[1] in my own Church. Practically everything one wants to see lies the other side of the reforms it envisages, or others like them. Nothing must delay us pushing out from that end and overhauling the existing machinery.

But when one has said this, and if one has any energies left (which is a very big question for a bishop or indeed for any minister or layman fully extended in the service of the institutional Church), one has got to get off one's coat, collar or mitre and begin from the other end also. For no amount of reform of the existing structure will in itself meet the needs of the new Reformation. And this start from the other side has virtually not yet begun. Practically everything we have done, and it *is* impressive, consists of probing operations, however adventurous, from our present church base. The difference of approach is very well brought out in a recent news-sheet from the Parishfield centre near Detroit,[2] which draws attention to the distinction between 'experimental' and 'exploratory' ministries, words that are often assumed to be synonymous and interchangeable:

[1] See, further, Eric James, *Beyond Paul* (*Prism* Pamphlet No. 19, 1964).
[2] *The Sword and Shield*, February-March 1964 (obtainable from Parishfield, Brighton, Michigan).

LIVING IN THE OVERLAP

Experimental ministries, with all their variations, share one assumption that the essential *form* of Christian mission and ministry is known. All presuppose some kind of congregation.... Many of the activities may take place apart from this gathering and may involve other than members; but the congregation is the center about which all aspects of the experiment revolve.

An *exploratory* ministry, on the other hand, presupposes no forms at all. The exploration is entered into precisely because those who undertake it do not presume to know in advance what the structures appropriate to ministry in the urban-industrial culture may be. They set out to explore the metropolitan complex (for example) as objectively as possible, seeking any evidence of ministry actually being performed there, prepared to acknowledge free and responsible servanthood in whatever form it may be found....

The danger to every exploratory ministry is that it will be preempted by the institution's demand for structure and 'results'. 'How many new church members has this activity produced?' is not just a crass caricature of the official attitude; it is the question that gnaws us all from within. We who are involved in exploration sympathize with the poor soul who wrote:

> 'I wish that my room had a floor.
> I don't so much care for a door;
>   But this crawling around
>   Without touching the ground
> Is getting to be quite a bore'.

Yet we know, at the same time, that the floor is *there*, and that the way to find it is not to pass prematurely through the door to experimentation....

At the moment, several open questions confront us: (1) Can the organized church afford to let some of its members engage in exploratory ministries while maintaining their 'good standing' in the institution? (2) Can exploratory ministries be effectively carried on as functions of the institution? (3) Have we been right in assuming that, still in our time, some form of 'fellowship' (*koinonia*) is indispensable to the Christian community? and, if so, *what does it look like*?

These are searching questions, and I certainly have no

confidence that I know the answers to them. But I am convinced that the Church has got to discover the answers by trying. I think we may be reasonably sure that the form of fellowship relevant to what Bonhoeffer called a genuinely 'worldly' life[1] is one that presupposes that the salt is at least 95 per cent of the time 'in solution'. It is the exact opposite of the 'enclosed' community—and this may be the equivalent of the 'dissolution' of the monasteries in the new Reformation. Five per cent of the year is in fact three weeks, and, split perhaps into a continuous fortnight and two week-ends, may represent the maximum that any Christian community or order engaged in the world should spend in being together as such.

With regard to the delicate relationship between the responsibility of the institution and the freedom of exploratory ministries, a question that is always with me personally is 'What would a missionary *bishop* look like in twentieth-century secular society?' Episcopalians (since their very name is at stake—though how glad I am we do not have to use it in England!) are perhaps more guilty of structural fundamentalism over bishops than anywhere else. Here, as with purely residential cures at the parish level, there needs to be a good shaking up of what Bishop Emrich of Michigan has called 'the one type-soldier assumption'.[2] By a missionary bishop, I mean one who is really exercising an exploratory and not only an experimental ministry—for one can be experimental, as far as time allows, at the moment. I suspect that it would begin by meaning that financially he should be part of the structure of society and not of the Church. In other words, he should be the episcopal equivalent of the priest-worker—which, indeed, I would see gradually becoming the normative pattern of ministry 'under the form of a servant'. His job would be the oversight and co-ordination, theologically and practically, of

---

[1] *Op. cit.*, p. 166.
[2] *Part-Time Priests?*, ed. Robin Denniston (Skeffington, London, 1960), p. 49. See my own essay, 'A New Model of Episcopacy', in *Bishops*, ed. the Bishop of Llandaff (Faith Press, London, 1961).

all those ministries which start 'from the other end'. But I believe that it is equally important, especially during the period of the overlap, that he should have one foot as firmly inside the organization of the Church as he has the other firmly outside. Indeed, symbolically it might be desirable that he should be paid half and half. For it is essential that the institution shall not be able to disown him—so that he becomes the odd man out and it can go on untroubled. Unless this kind of initiative can take place with the authority of the institution at the very same time as it gives him his freedom, the new Reformation will not get started from both ends at once. And what is focused in the person of the bishop, the *servus servorum Dei*, to use the Pope's fine title, must be made genuinely representative of all ministry, ordained or lay, within the servant Church.

Can the Church work from both ends like this without breaking in the middle? Can its right hand respect, even when it does not know, what its left hand is doing? This will be the test of its unity in the period ahead of us. Division denominationally is not, I trust, likely to be the threat of the new Reformation. Division and disintegration within each denomination, each local church, and indeed each Christian, produced by the strain of living in the overlap is an all too present possibility. Can the Church survive it? My faith is that it can—just. And that is why I believe in a new Reformation as a real and exciting divine possibility.

But let us not underestimate the cost. To state it I cannot do better than close with some further words of Albert van den Heuvel:

> Let those who are satisfied with the old structure live in it, but let them not hinder the others from working out their calling in today's world. Let those who worship happily on Sundays do so happily, but let them not hinder the others who live their *koinonia* in less traditional forms and on less traditional days. Let those who can still stand the heat of the day with their traditional confessions of faith do so, but let them rejoice in those who are for the total rethinking of all they know. Let not those who know

laugh at those who do not know much any longer. The unity of the Church has to be kept between the traditionalists (in the best sense of that word) and the renewers. Both can claim legitimacy in the community of Jesus, but both should recognize that they exist by the grace of the other!

POSTSCRIPT

> 'Watchman, what of the night?
> Watchman, what of the night?'
> The watchman says:
> 'Morning comes, and also the night.
> If you will inquire, inquire;
> Come back again.'[1]

WHAT, then, is the prospect for the Church? Outwardly it is an enigma, inwardly a mystery. All one can be sure of is that it is bound to be morning *and* night, darkness *and* dawn.

Speaking simply from within the situation one knows in England, I become increasingly convinced that the flags of dawn are likely to appear only out of a night a good deal darker yet. For it is not only academic theology which has been living on its own fat. The supply of fat is running out also for the Church. It will be a night in which the presuppositions of Christendom, of a traditional power-backed Establishment, are likely to vanish at an accelerating pace. The politeness, the respect, the goodwill on which the Church as an institution has been able to presume—and from which it has sought to impose the terms of the debate, culturally and morally—are visibly dissolving. The fat, represented still, for instance, by the inflated figures for infant baptism, could easily be cut by fifty per cent in a generation.[2] Christenings could quickly go the way of 'churchings', which when I was ordained twenty years ago were still part of the religious ethos of working-class England. Compulsory religion in schools will scarcely survive the next major reform, and there is no reason to suppose that religious broadcasting will for ever enjoy its protected 'slot'.

---

[1] Isaiah 21.11-12.
[2] In the eight years between 1956 and 1962 the baptism figures for the Church of England fell by nearly 12% and for the London area by over 20%.

None of this is necessarily a bad thing. I am not depressed by it (or, if I am honest, I say I am not). What depresses me much more is the possible reaction of churchmen. It could lead to a further withdrawal inside the camp. It could result in carrying on gamely until the structures collapse, thus proving the Marxists right (that ultimately we accept change only under economic pressure) and depriving ourselves of any spiritual benefits of doing the right thing for the right reasons. Or, much more commonly, it is likely to be met by accusations that such talk merely causes despondency and aggravates the decline, that the situation is never as black as it is painted (which it isn't), and that with more faithfulness, more time, and the doubling of ordinands urged by Leslie Paul,[1] the front can be held and people 'got back'. Such was the dominant clerical reaction I received to the recent article in *The Observer* colour supplement[2] by Nick Stacey, the Rector of Woolwich. 'It may be true, but why wash our dirty linen in public?' 'At least it has taught us some things to avoid.' The assumption was fundamentally that the system is the best we've got, that we must make it work—and that it doesn't help to be stabbed in the back.

I find this reaction, however understandable, more depressing than the disease. For, when every discount has been made (for personality, dog-collars, beards, arrogance, impatience, false criteria of 'success', etc.), I believe the account in that article is fundamentally correct, and that it is not until we have worked through to the point at which it ends (even if in some places it may be a generation or more away) that there is real hope. So far from finding the article depressing (which it was), I regard it and the situation it describes as one of the 'signs', to which I shall be referring, that the Church exists to offer to the world in this generation.

Up till now, particularly in a country like England, we have assumed that the Church exists to create a settled pattern within which everyone, if he wishes to, can lead the Christian

[1] *Op. cit.*, ch. IX.
[2] 'A Mission's Failure', December 6, 1964.

life. The basis of the parish system is that there is a building and a priest within walking distance of every Englishman. The Church of England operates a national 'network' and its first obligation is to maintain this coverage and to keep the system supplied. I should be the last to suggest that it retract from its national responsibilities. I believe it should be more exposed to the whole life of the nation. What I doubt is whether it does this in any convincing way by putting ninety per cent of its resources into maintaining a network of residential centres, on the assumption that the home is the point from which the rest of life is influenced. This last assumption is palpably untrue: the influences from other centres of power *on* the home are far more potent than the other way round. The decisive power-centres of the modern world are not included in the net at all (except in the purely nominal sense that even Transport House, the B.B.C. Television Centre and the Ford Motor Works are in somebody's parish). Moreover, by attempting to cover the waterfront and keep a service station going everywhere, singularly few signs are *in fact* being shown to convince those outside the religious circle that the Church has a relevance or a future. Time was when this was the way to witness to the presence of the Kingdom. I am far from saying that we should simply contract out of this pattern, even if we could. I am sure that we should keep a skeleton service going everywhere, so that no one need be out of range of ministry (and ecumenically if we pooled our resources this—and more—would be easy). But this should not be the only or even the main thrust of our witness.

Taking a cue from Colin Williams's second book *What in the World?*, which I found even more exciting than his first but which unfortunately arrived on my desk too late to be incorporated into the substance of this book, I would say that the primary task of the Church is to produce not settlements, but 'signs'. The Son of Man himself existed to be a 'sign'[1] to 'this generation', a sign of the Kingdom, of what God was doing in its midst, and all his 'works' pointed to this. Similarly,

[1] Luke 11.30.

the Church exists to be the sign, the first-fruits, of the New Humanity. As Colin Williams says:[1]

> Where we see the promise of the dividing walls of hostility being broken down; where we see the promise of widening participation in the open community of the New Humanity; where we see the drive towards the opening of the creative possibilities of life to those formerly excluded; there we see the presence of Christ working out his purpose; and the call of Christ for the presence of his followers. We are to read the 'signs of the times'; we are to ask for the gifts of the Spirit which will enable us to discern the presence of God in the events of history and will enable us to be witnesses who by word and deed seek to bring the world to a recognition of its living Lord.

Where these things are happening, in the midst of all the ambiguities of the 'secular hope' of our day, there Christ is and there the Church should be. Is the Church *free* enough to be there, to let itself 'take shape around his servant presence in the world'?[2] That is the crucial question for the new Reformation. Thank God there are 'parables' of what this presence means. One thinks instinctively of what Trevor Huddleston, Martin Luther King, Abbé Pierre, Fr Borelli, the East Harlem Protestant Parish, the Notting Hill Housing Association and numerous others have come to stand for. They are 'signs' to yet another generation that the Church has a future, that with God things are possible that with politicians are impossible. When men see these things they lift up their heads and drop their cynicism about the Church. The young are encouraged to believe that there may yet be hope. It is significant that the immediate examples that come to mind have very little to do with the traditional parochial structure of the Church. But there is plenty even within the diocese I serve to show that from that end too ensigns of hope can be set up—so that 'Southwark' has become not only a by-word but a sign for many. On another front I shall be content if *Honest to God* may in a small way be seen as such a sign, such a parable of witness.

[1] *Op. cit.*, p. 62. [2] *Op. cit.*, p. 46.

POSTSCRIPT

All these things are only parables: they do not 'add up'—to a new Reformation or to anything else. Sometimes they are as small as a man's hand. They take shape round the areas of human need—whether of man's strength or weakness—wherever the Spirit of the Lord is. And where that is, there is liberty[1] and there is hope. If the Church is to witness to the open future of mankind in Christ, these are the points at which it must allow far more of its resources to find release—and not leave the other things undone.

The night comes—but also the morning. Is there to be a new Reformation? 'If you will inquire, inquire.' But to the puzzled or the sceptical I would urge, Do not merely inquire. Give yourself—'at the perilous moving edges of change'.[2] And then 'come back again'.

[1] II Corinthians 3.17.
[2] Colin Williams, *op. cit.*, p. 4.

Appendix I

CAN A TRULY CONTEMPORARY PERSON *NOT* BE AN ATHEIST?

A bishop lecturing on atheism still strikes people, in England at any rate, as incongruous—though since I have freely been called 'the atheist bishop' (as well as plenty of other things!) many will simply assume that I have now reached my proper level. Indeed, I have discovered at least one virtue in what I believe to be the unhappy German title of *Honest to God*, *Gott ist Anders* (God is Different). A friend of mine found that he was able to take as many copies as he liked to East Germany— they thought it was atheistic propaganda!

In fact I want to treat the question of atheism as a very serious one for those of us who would call ourselves Christians. So I have deliberately posed it, for myself as well as for you, in the form: 'Can a truly contemporary person *not* be an atheist?' For I believe there is an important sense in which a person who is fully a man of our times *must*—or, at any rate, *may*—be an atheist before he can be a Christian. That is to say, there is so much in the atheist's case which is true that for many people today the only Christian faith which can be valid *for them* is one that takes over *post mortem dei*, after the death of God as 'God' has traditionally been understood. I put this strongly—and can afford to put it strongly—as I shall insist equally strongly on the faith. But it is a faith which I suspect for increasing numbers of our contemporaries will only be possible through, and out the other side of, the atheist critique. The Christian should therefore take atheism seriously, not only so that he may be able to 'answer' it, but so that he himself may still be able to be a believer in the mid-twentieth century.

With this in mind, I would ask you to expose yourselves to the three thrusts of modern atheism. These are not so much three types of atheism—each is present, in varying degree, in any representative type—so much as three motives which have impelled men, particularly over the past hundred years, to question the God of their upbringing and ours. They may be represented by three summary statements:

1. God is intellectually superfluous.
2. God is emotionally dispensable.
3. God is morally intolerable.

Let us consider each of them in turn.

1. *God is intellectually superfluous*

'I have no need of that hypothesis': so Laplace, the great astronomer, replied to Napoleon, when asked where God fitted into his system. Within the terms of an astronomical system, he was clearly correct. To bring in God to fill the gaps in our science or to deal with life at the point at which things get beyond human explanation or control is intellectual laziness or practical superstition. And yet, ever since the scientific and technological revolution which created our modern world, the defence of Christianity has in fact been bound up with staving off the advance of secularization, whose effect is precisely to close the gaps in the circle of explanation and control. Bonhoeffer put it accurately enough in the well-known passage in his *Letters*:[1]

> Man has learned to cope with all questions of importance without recourse to God as a working hypothesis. In questions concerning science, art, and even ethics, this has become an understood thing which one scarcely dares to tilt at any more. But for the last hundred years or so it has become increasingly true of religious questions also: it is becoming evident that everything gets along without 'God', and just as well as before. As in the scientific field, so in human affairs generally, what we call

[1] *Letters and Papers from Prison*, pp. 145-6.

'God' is being more and more edged out of life, losing more and more ground. . . .

Christian apologetic has taken the most varying forms of opposition to this self-assurance. Efforts are made to prove to a world thus come of age that it cannot live without the tutelage of 'God'. Even though there has been a surrender on all secular problems, there still remain the so-called ultimate questions—death, guilt—on which only 'God' can furnish an answer, and which are the reason why God and the Church and the pastor are needed. . . . But what if one day they no longer exist as such, if they too can be answered without 'God'?

One has only to raise this question to recognize the threat that most churchmen instinctively feel and the vested interest which we still have in the 'God of the gaps'. Indeed, when we hear it from the atheist, we take it as the attack for which it is clearly intended. Here, for instance, is Sir Julian Huxley:[1]

The god hypothesis is no longer of any pragmatic value for the interpretation or comprehension of nature, and indeed often stands in the way of better and truer interpretation. . . .

It will soon be as impossible for an intelligent, educated man or woman to believe in a god as it is now to believe that the earth is flat, that flies can be spontaneously generated, that disease is a divine punishment, or that death is always due to witchcraft.

God is an 'x' in the equation whom we cannot get on without, a cause, controller or designer whom we are bound to posit or allow room for—this hypothesis seems to men today more and more superfluous. There is nothing indeed that *disproves* it. It is simply, in the words of Anthony Flew, the linguistic philosopher, being 'killed by inches'; it is dying 'the death of a thousand qualifications'. And he vividly illustrates how this happens in the parable[2] from which Paul van Buren starts his *Secular Meaning of the Gospel*:[3]

[1] *Religion without Revelation* (Max Parrish, London, 2nd ed. 1957), pp. 58 and 62.
[2] *New Essays in Philosophical Theology*, ed. A. G. N. Flew and A. C. MacIntyre (SCM Press, London, and Macmillan, New York, 1955), pp. 96-7.
[3] P. 3.

> Once upon a time two explorers came upon a clearing in the jungle. In the clearing were growing many flowers and many weeds. One explorer says, 'Some gardener must tend this plot.' The other disagrees. 'There is no gardener.' So they pitch their tents and set a watch. No gardener is ever seen. 'But perhaps he is an invisible gardener.' So they set up a barbed wire fence. They electrify it. They patrol it with bloodhounds. . . . But no shrieks ever suggest that some intruder has received a shock. No movement of the wire ever betrays an invisible climber. The bloodhounds never give cry. Yet still the Believer is not convinced. 'But there is a gardener, invisible, intangible, insensible to electric shocks, a gardener who has no scent and makes no sound, a gardener who comes secretly to look after the garden which he loves.' At last the Sceptic despairs, 'But what is left of your original assertion? Just how does what you call an invisible, intangible, eternally elusive gardener differ from an imaginary gardener or even from no gardener at all?'

And what is true at the level of explanation is equally true at the level of control. Neither to account for sickness nor to deal with it does it occur to men today to bring in 'God'. Or if it does occur to them, it is when they have reached the end of their tether and 'turn to prayer'. But this simply confirms the judgment of Werner Pelz that 'When we use the word "God" we are talking about something which no longer connects with anything in most people's life, except with whatever happens to be left over when all the vital connections have been made.'[1] Most of us today are practical atheists. The 'god-hypothesis' is as irrelevant for running an economy or coping with the population explosion as it was for Laplace's system. As a factor you must take into account in the practical business of living, God is 'out'—and no amount of religious manipulation can force him back in. He is peripheral, redundant, incredible—and therefore *as God* displaced: in Julian Huxley's words, 'not a ruler, but the last fading smile of a cosmic Cheshire Cat'.[2]

I am very far from saying this is the whole truth or that all the atheist's arguments on this front, or any other, are valid

[1] *Prism*, April 1963, p. 23. [2] *Op. cit.*, p. 58.

(many of them reflect a very superficial or crudely tendentious understanding even of the traditional theology). What I am urging is that we allow ourselves to feel the full force of this attack rather than spend our time looking for yet another hole in the wire fence.

2. *God is emotionally dispensable*

The reference earlier to Bonhoeffer's theme of man come of age shows the close connection. Man is discovering that he no longer *needs* God or religion. He finds he can stand on his own feet without having to refer constantly to Daddy in the background or to run to Mummy's apron-strings.

According to this line of attack religion is a prop or a sop. It is not merely something incredible and superfluous: it is a dangerous illusion which can prevent men facing reality and shouldering responsibility. This lies at the heart of the Freudian critique of religion as the universal neurosis or the Marxist attack on it as 'the opium of the people'. God and the gods are the projection of men's fears, insecurities and longings. They act as a debilitating crutch which men must have the courage to discard if they are to grow up and shake off the sense of helplessness which religion both induces and sanctions.

The call of atheism here is to man to cut the strings, to move out of the shadow of the Father-figure, to cease treating God as a peg, or a refuge, or a compensation for miseries which he should be fighting. Secularization means that man must accept responsibility for his own destiny, neither trying to blame it on the gods nor expecting some providence to relieve him of it or see him through.

Again I believe we must recognize the essential truth of this attack. Whatever as Christians we may wish to add or come back with, we should not be caught trying to defend this God or save him from death by artificial respiration. This was the strength of Bonhoeffer's courageous acceptance of the edging out of the 'God of religion': unless a man is prepared to be 'forsaken' by that God, he cannot find what Jesus is showing us on the Cross. But are we prepared to let that God go? In varying degrees we all *need* religion, and nowhere more than here is the thrust of atheism seen as a threat. The tearing down of the traditional structure in which 'the good Lord provides' and surrounds the whole of life with the protective comfort of the womb is viewed as an act of sacrilege which must be withstood, if not for our own sake, at any rate for the sake of the weaker brethren to whose pastoral care we hasten. Or, as an alternative line of defence, we seek to dismiss those who try, as someone has put it, to 'destroy my grandmother's religion with my grandfather's science'. But if we are honest, our 'grandmother's religion' probably plays a much larger role in our conscious and unconscious life than we care to admit.

Consider, for instance, the quite central belief in Providence. The trust that in and through and despite everything there meets one a love, stronger than death, from which nothing can separate is fundamental to the Christian confidence. But I am sure there are some forms of belief in providence which merely pander to emotional immaturity. And these are the forms which secretly retain God in the gaps of our ignorance or fears, or which see him as a celestial manipulator rearranging, interrupting, or taking over from, the forces which would otherwise be at work. And when these forces are those of human responsibility their 'providential overruling' can quickly lead to the debilitation, the superstition, and even the fatalism, of which the atheists accuse the religious.

Each time I go to London Airport I am met by a large notice, greeting me with the assurance: 'BOAC takes good care of you.' What are we to make of this declaration of secular providence? If it fails, whom are we to blame— BOAC or God? When first I flew, I used to indulge in additional 'cover' for those tense thirty seconds of take-off as one waits to see whether the plane will make it and leave the ground. Did my prayer in the gap—when somehow a little supernatural 'lift' would always be welcome—do credit to my trust in God? I think not. I suspect that this is where a Christian *ought* to be a practical atheist—and trust the pilot. If this is the sort of God he believes in—and logically he should only believe in him if he is a God who *does* take over—then the protest of the atheist is valid. Men need to be weaned, however painfully, from refusal to accept the burden of responsibility. A God who relieves them of this requires killing.

This clamour for the death of a God who keeps men languid and dispossessed, associated with Feuerbach before Marx, Engels and Freud developed it in their different ways, leads directly into the even more strident protest which expresses itself in the third statement.

3. *God is morally intolerable*

This reverses Voltaire's dictum that 'If God did not exist, we should have to invent him'. It says rather, 'If God did exist, we should have to abolish him.' This is the tradition that derives again from Feuerbach, and runs through Bakunin, Proudhon and Nietzsche to Camus and Sartre. It represents the real quick of twentieth-century atheism, in contrast with its dying nerves—if one may dare to thus speak of Marxism, as I think one can, as somewhat dated. It is what Jacques Maritain has called[1] 'positive atheism'. It centres in the determination that God must *die* if man is to *live*. It is not content with accepting the negative absence of God and carrying on as though everything remained the same. It is concerned positively in living in 'a world without God'—creating the justice and the meaning and the freedom which God, the great blood-sucker, has drained away.

But we should be careful not to state it in too emotive language. It would be easy to discredit this whole protest as the titanism of a Nietzsche or the outburst of a few intellectuals. But if this was once true, it is certainly true no longer. Camus spoke for an entire emerging generation. There is a dispassionate quality about modern atheism, of a piece with our whole urban-secular civilization. It is not vindictive or despairing, and it is noticeably losing its overtones of an anti-

[1] 'The Meaning of Contemporary Atheism', *The Listener*, 9 March 1950.

religion. A speaker can deliberately ask to be introduced on the television, as happened in my presence, as an 'atheist' rather than an 'agnostic' without any sense of defiance. And this I believe is a healthy development. For in 'the secular city' constructive debate will only become possible if atheism, like Christianity, can discover what it means to be 'religionless', and the various competing 'ologies' and 'isms' are 'de-sacralized'.

This is not in the least to suggest that this particular form of atheism, above all, should lapse into indifferentism. It has a moral nerve which must not be cut, if it is to continue to purge and purify. For it draws its strength from the seriousness with which it takes the problem of evil. A God who 'causes' or 'allows' the suffering of a single child is morally intolerable. So the debate ranges, back and forth, in some of the great dialogues of modern literature—in Dostoievski's *Brothers Karamazov*, in Camus's *The Plague* and, most recently, in Peter de Vries's *The Blood of the Lamb*[1] (describing the agony of a father watching his girl die of leukemia). But, of course, this is no intellectuals' debate. It is the root of atheism in most ordinary people, and today it is openly asserted even by the young. Here, for instance, is a girl of 19 interviewed in the *Daily Mirror*:[2]

'Do you believe in God?'

'No. I used to, but not now. I don't see how there can be a benevolent God. There are too many tragedies—personal and in the world. . . . RELIGION IS DISGUSTING.'

Religion is disgusting. God does not solve the problem of suffering: he only magnifies it. To push off evil on to God simply makes him into a Devil—and in any case represents a cowardly evasion. Men must carry the can and refuse the temptation to dissociation or transference.

I believe that this is a profoundly moral response, and one that must be taken with the utmost seriousness. Any glib

[1] Little, Brown and Co., Boston, and Gollancz, London, 1961.
[2] In a brilliant piece of reporting by Marjorie Proops, 'For These Girls, It's All Happening', 5 March 1964.

notion of a God who 'causes' cancer or 'sends' the streptococcus *is* a blasphemy. Most traditional theodicy, so far from justifying the ways of God to man, has the effect of strengthening atheism. 'Whatever your sickness is', the priest is instructed to say in the seventeenth-century Anglican *Book of Common Prayer*, 'know certainly that it is God's visitation.' Who could speak like that today? Atheism has done its purifying work. For there is nothing that provokes our generation to doubt or blasphemy more than the idea of a Being who sends such events into the lives of individuals. One of the liberating effects of secularization is that *this* idea of divine causation has at any rate been discredited. People rightly look for natural rather than supernatural causes. *But they still assume that Christians teach otherwise*—and their God is dismissed with them with indignation and disgust.

After the Death of God

Can a truly contemporary person *not* be an atheist? It is a very real question. Not all people will feel the force of each of these thrusts. Their God may survive any or indeed all of them. I would certainly not want to suggest that a contemporary Christian *must* go through the mill of first being an atheist. But I firmly believe that he *may*, and that increasingly many will.

But *post mortem dei*, what? Is, in fact, faith possible out the other side? I believe that it is, and that not merely despite the death of God but even because of it. For this, after all, is no new situation for the people of God. The faith of Abraham, the father of faith, was born, as St Paul reminds us,[1] out of 'contemplating his own body, now as good as dead, and the deadness of Sarah's womb'. The faith of Job was possible to him only after all that he trusted in had first been removed. Even Jesus himself had to go through the process of the death of God—of the One who allowed it all to happen, 'with a million angels watching, and they never move a wing'.[2] But,

[1] Romans 4.17-25.
[2] From *Friday Morning*, in *9 Carols or Ballads* by Sydney Carter. (Clarion Photographic Services Ltd, London, 1964).

APPENDIX I

above all, Christianity itself was 'born in the grave' (some of you may know the remarkable little sermon of that title in Tillich's *Shaking of the Foundations*[1]): it could only come into being at all *post mortem dei*. And for each one of us in some degree the Resurrection can only happen after the death of God. Though it looks as if everything is taken away—even the body of the Lord—yet this is not the destruction of Christianity but its liberation.

For—with all metaphysical security shattered, with even the word 'God' of doubtful currency, with no theodicy of our own that we can establish[2]—we find that we still cannot get shot of God: after his death he is disturbingly alive. No one that I know has wrestled through this problem more compellingly in our day than William Hamilton of Colgate Rochester Divinity School, New York. His *New Essence of Christianity* seeks in an age of theological 'reduction' to lay claim to those few things that are certain, and in a chapter called 'Belief in a Time of the Death of God' he writes:[3]

> In one sense God seems to have withdrawn from the world and its sufferings, and this leads us to accuse him of either irrelevance or cruelty. But in another sense, he is experienced as a pressure and a wounding from which we would love to be free. For many of us who call ourselves Christians, therefore, believing in the time of the 'death of God' means that he is there when we do not want him, in ways we do not want him, and he is not there when we do want him.

Is not the situation of many of us today that we feel we *must* be atheists, and yet we *cannot* be atheists? God as we have been led to posit him *is* intellectually superfluous, *is* emotionally dispensable, *is* morally intolerable—and yet, in grace and demand, he *will not* let us go. The hound of heaven still dogs us, the 'beyond in our midst' still encounters us, when all the images, all the projections, even all the words, for God have been broken.

---
[1] Scribner, New York, 1948, and SCM Press, London, 1949, pp. 164-8.
[2] Romans 10.3.
[3] P. 69.

Can a truly contemporary person *not* be an atheist? In one sense, he can hardly fail to be. There is no going back to the pre-secular view of the world, where God is always 'there' to be brought in, run to, or blamed. Yet, in another sense, he may find that he *cannot* be an atheist, however much he would like to be. For on the Emmaus road, on the way back from the tomb, the risen Christ comes up with him and he knows himself constrained.

What then, in the last analysis, remains the difference between the atheist and the one who cannot finally rest in that name? In *Honest to God* I wrote:[1]

> So conditioned for us is the word 'God' by association with a Being out there [with all, in other words, that the anti-theist finds superfluous, dispensable or intolerable] that Tillich warns us . . . 'You must forget everything traditional you have learned about God, perhaps even that word itself.'[2] Indeed, the line between those who believe in God and those who do not bears little relation to their profession of the existence or non-existence of such a Being. It is a question, rather, of their openness to the holy, the sacred, in the unfathomable depths of even the most secular relationship. As Martin Buber puts it of the person who professedly denies God, 'When he, too, who abhors the name, and believes himself to be godless, gives his whole being to addressing the Thou of his life, as a Thou that cannot be limited by another, he addresses God.'[3]

There, I suggest, lies the clue to the real difference. Let me use a familiar analogy. In dealing with other people it is possible for us to treat them simply as things—to use them, control them, manipulate them. This is what John Macmurray[4] calls the *instrumental* relationship. Or, if for no other reason than that we soon discover they are not wholly amenable to such treatment, we can relate ourselves to them in what he calls the *functional* relationship, of co-operation with them.

[1] Pp. 47-8.
[2] *The Shaking of the Foundations*, p. 64.
[3] *I and Thou*. English translation by R. Gregor Smith (T. and T. Clark, Edinburgh, and Scribner, New York, 1937), p. 76.
[4] In *Interpreting the Universe*, Faber and Faber, London, 1936.

This is the most common relation we have with others, in which we treat them often as means to an end but never merely as means. But, thirdly, we can give ourselves to them in pure *personal* relationship, responding to them in love and trust for their own sakes. And ultimately it is only in this relationship that we can know them—and we ourselves be known—*as persons*.

To transfer this analogy to the universe, to life as a whole, we can respond to it in a purely instrumental, scientific relationship—at the level of its mathematical regularities. We can regard reality as ultimately nothing more than a collocation of atoms, and we can even try to run history as a piece of social engineering. But there are few purely mechanistic materialists today. Much more common are those whose ultimate frame of reference is a functional one—humanists, whether dialectical, evolutionary or idealistic. And the atheist is the man who in his attitude to life stops there—for whom nothing finally is absolute or unconditional, for whom all is a means (though not merely a means).

The man who finds himself compelled to acknowledge the reality of *God*, whatever he may call him or however he may image him, is the man who, through the mathematical regularities and through the functional values, is met by the same grace and the same claim that he recognizes in the I-Thou relation with another person. It may come to him through nature, through the claims of artistic integrity or scientific truth, through the engagements of social justice or of personal communion. Yet always it comes with an overmastering givenness and demand such as no other thing or person has the power to convey or the right to require. Like the child Samuel in the Temple, confusing the call of God with the voice of Eli, he may think at first that it can simply be identified with or contained within the finite relationship by which it is mediated. He may not be able to tell what to make of it, he may find it profoundly disturbing, but he knows it in the end to be inescapable and unconditional. In this relationship, too, he discovers himself known and judged and accepted for what ultimately he is. He finds in it for himself the way, the truth and the life. And if he is a Christian, he recognizes and acknowledges this grace and claim supremely in the person of Jesus Christ, the definition at one and the same time of a genuinely human existence and of this intangible, ineffable reality of 'God'. He agrees, passionately, with the atheist that such a reality cannot be *used* or *needed*. A God like that *is* superfluous, dispensable, intolerable. In fact it is *no God*. And then, when that God is dead, the Lord appears.

The Lord appears—not as one who is needed, nor as one who intrudes, forcing men's freedom or curtailing their responsibility, but as one who 'makes as though he would go further'.[1] Like the disciples on the road to Emmaus, we find ourselves faced with the bewildering double adjustment of learning at one and the same time to live in a world without God and in a world with God. It is a new situation, a post-resurrection world, in which the old *is* dead. There is no question of introducing that God again by the back door or of returning to the *status quo ante*. Yet, despite the irreversibility of that change, there is the constraint of the other reality with which to come to terms. How, then, does it stand in relation to three thrusts we examined before?

In the first place, God remains intellectually superfluous, in the sense that he does not need to be 'brought in'. There is no 'place' for him in the system—or for that matter on its edge. The ring has been closed in which before an opening was left for God. Secularization must be gladly accepted—and no attempt made to find another hole in the fence or to reinstate him outside it.

There is a parallel here, to return to our previous analogy, with attempts to 'locate' the element of the distinctively personal—the free, spiritual reality of 'I' and 'Thou'—in our description of human behaviour. Clearly this does not depend on establishing gaps in the chemistry or the psychology. Efforts to secure a place for freedom and the spirit in that way are foredoomed. Nor is there any more hope in representing it

[1] Luke 24.28.

APPENDIX I

as external to a closed system, which a free spirit, depicted as a sort of super-natural self, controls and directs from the outside—though such a model has been a common presupposition both in psychology and theology. To know a man as a person is not to posit another invisible factor between or beyond the regularities which the scientist investigates. It is to respond to a total reality which engages one in, through and under the regularities, which in no way denies them and yet is related to them like another dimension.

Similarly with God. As a factor introduced to make the system work he is redundant. In that sense it is possible to answer every question without God—even the ones that before were thought to admit only of a religious solution. And at the level of control things get along, for good or for ill, just as well without him. It is not necessary to bring him in.

But in another sense it is not possible to leave him out—any more than it is possible to run an economy or cope with the population explosion without in the last analysis treating persons as persons, without reckoning with the dimension of the 'Thou'. God is a reality of life whom one cannot ultimately evade. Huxley, quite legitimately, may not need him as a hypothesis, nor Flew be able to trap him in his mesh. Like the scientist or philosopher who looks in vain for the 'Thou' in the person he is analysing without addressing, the searcher for God finds himself in the position of Job:[1]

> Behold, I go forward, but he is not there;
> and backward, but I cannot perceive him;
> on the left hand I seek him, but I cannot behold him;
> I turn to the right hand, but I cannot see him.

But then he adds, aware of the presence by which all the while he is being explored:

> But he knows the way that I take.

The one who is superfluous as a hypothesis becomes all too present as a subject in encounter.

[1] Job 23.8-10.

Then, secondly, God continues to be emotionally dispensable. The returning Lord does not come as compensation for the gap left by the God of the gaps. There is no solace to restore the old relationships. The crutches are broken, and it remains 'good for you that I go away'.[1] Nothing relieves of responsibility those who have to live by the Spirit.

Yet man come of age is still called to be a son. It is a mark of our religious immaturity that the 'Father' image inextricably suggests emotional dependence, if not domination. The son never seems to grow up. Yet in fact for the New Testament 'sonship' is a figure for freedom and stands precisely for man who has passed out of his minority and come of age.[2] The Christian faith, so far from seeking to keep men in strings, calls them to maturity, not the maturity of the adolescent revolting *against* a father, but of the 'full-grown man' entering into the responsible freedom of the son and heir.

There is nothing in the God of the New Testament—nor indeed in the God who said to the prophet,[3] 'Son of man, stand upon your feet and I will speak with you'—which would keep men languid or dispossessed. The call is to bear and to share the terrible freedom of love. And faith in the fatherly reality to which sonship is the response is not a belief in anything that undercuts this. Speaking of a mature trust in providence, Tillich writes:[4]

> The man who believes in providence does not believe that a special divine activity will alter the conditions of finitude and estrangement. He believes, and asserts with the courage of faith, that no situation whatsoever can frustrate the fulfilment of his ultimate destiny, that nothing can separate him from the love of God which is in Jesus Christ.

And again:[5]

> Providence means that there is a creative and saving possibility

---

[1] John 16.7.
[2] See especially John 8.31-8 and Galatians 4.1-7.
[3] Ezekiel 2.1.
[4] *Systematic Theology*, vol. i, p. 296.
[5] *The Shaking of the Foundations*, p. 106.

implied in every situation, which cannot be destroyed by any event.

The prayer that is immature is the prayer that cannot trust this, but resorts to reliance on physical or mental interference. True prayer is not for additional 'cover' that, if the worst comes to the worst, the controls may be taken over by celestial manipulation. True prayer is prayer for the pilot, and by the pilot, that his responsibility may be heightened, not diminished, by trusting the love his life exists to serve and from which not even 'the worst' can separate.

This brings us, lastly, to the third charge, that God is morally intolerable. Again, it is a charge that stands. A Being who 'sends' the worst into the lives of individuals or who stands aside to 'permit' it is a God who must die. But that is precisely what the Christian faith proclaims happened at Calvary. The God who could have sent 'twelve legions of angels' and did not is exposed as the God who failed even his Son. The obituary read by the atheist is valid, even if sometimes shrill.

Nothing in the Christian faith implies the rehabilitation of that God. Yet the Christian, as he looks back on the Cross from the other side of the Resurrection, sees not a world without God at its borders but a world with God at its centre. What it means to believe in love as the final reality is to be discerned not in the absentee controller who allows the suffering but in the crucified transfiguring figure who bears it. The New Testament 'answer' to the problem of evil is given, not majestically out of the whirlwind[1] but agonizingly out of the darkness. As Bonhoeffer saw,[2] in that situation 'only a suffering God can help'. The God of the Christian faith, who alone can be 'our' God, can ultimately be revealed and responded to only as love which *takes* responsibility for evil—transformingly and victoriously.

For men to adjust to life in a world with that as its central reality is no intellectual exercise: it is, in Bonhoeffer's words

[1] Job 38.1.
[2] *Letters and Papers from Prison*, p. 164.

again,[1] to 'range themselves with God in his suffering'. That is the test he saw distinguishing Christians from unbelievers. And even among professed unbelievers there may at the point of dereliction, where the choice of our ultimate allegiance stands forth most starkly, be many who find that they cannot rail.

'For Christians, heathens alike he hangeth dead.'[2] Such is the reality Bonhoeffer recognized as the common presupposition of our age—replacing what he called 'the religious premise'. Atheists and Christians start there together. And on their walk from the tomb, sharing the disenchantment of other more facile hopes, the dialogue can begin.

[1] *Op. cit.*, p. 166.
[2] From his last poem, 'Christians and Unbelievers', *op. cit.*, pp. 166-7.

Appendix II

SPIRITUAL EDUCATION IN A WORLD WITHOUT RELIGION

Ruth Robinson

I have sometimes been asked recently: 'What effect has *Honest to God* and all the reaction to it had on your children?' The simple answer is—practically none at all. Life goes on much as it did before. The vital questions continue to be 'Do you have to go out tonight?', 'What can I wear for the party?', and 'What's for supper?' No one seems to have been shaken by the less friendly references to father in the newspapers: they have just been shrugged off and taken for granted. In fact, Stephen's comment one morning as he thumbed through the correspondence section of the *New Statesman* just about catches the family's assessment of the situation: 'Gosh, Daddy! Someone has said something nice about you in a newspaper!' Only once has shame and disapproval been expressed about what father has said in public. This was when he appeared obviously not to know that one of the Beatles was married. This they felt would take some living down!

No—the question for me is not 'What effect has the book had on the family?' but 'What effect has the family had on the book?', and this has been considerable. For it has been in the attempt to share and communicate our deepest convictions about life with our children, on their wave-length, that we have been forced time and again to ask ourselves, 'Is this what I really believe?' In the sphere of psychiatry, we recognize that much of what we know of the working of the human mind we have learnt from the earliest emotional reactions of infants. For myself, at least, there has come a clearer perception of what makes *me* tick spiritually from having for the last sixteen years been nurtured in a school in which they have been the teachers.

Communicating with Children

I have been asked to talk about 'Non-religious education'. This does not mean, for me at any rate, that I want to bring up my children without a sense of wonder and mystery, awe and reverence. On the contrary, I want as a parent to provide the soil of experience in which these spiritual seeds can germinate, so that later—much later, and without forcing—they may blossom into conscious commitment and response. But I do not want to cheat them of a spiritual reality within the scope of their experience, even when they are small, by dressing it up in 'religious' categories which may be real for me (because I am grown up and can think in abstract terms) but not for them. Grace and benediction can be realities for them in their closest personal relationships; wonder and mystery surround them in the real world of clockwork and coloured pictures, of snow and spring flowers, or of new baby brothers and sisters. Let us nurture these realities at the point where they are real *for them* and not divert them on to a pious side-road, however well-paved with good intentions.

Much of what I shall say will be concerned with language, with the words we use to give body to our thoughts and to share them with others. But human language is not confined to the spoken word, though this is a large part of it. We communicate with each other at a much deeper level even before our minds can conceive the thought or our tongues produce the speech. Our actions and attitudes, our choices and responses, what we don't say as much as what we do—all that we are speaks the living word between man and man in terms of flesh and blood. It becomes part of our inner 'knowledge' whether our conscious minds are involved or not. For a Christian all language is focused in the living Word, the man Jesus, who in terms of flesh and blood spelt out for us the meaning of our life, not only by what he said but by what he was. Our task as parents is to help our children to 'hear' this living Word for themselves and to hear it as naturally as breathing or sleeping, below the conscious level. And we must make sure that our spoken language, our explanations and definitions, make it easier, not harder, for them to hear with the inner ear this Word of life.

But first let us consider the actual spoken words we use. A Christian parent said to me recently, 'But a child's first questions are metaphysical ones', by which he meant that they need a religious answer. But do they? The child asks: 'Who made the world? How did it get here?', and we answer simply but glibly: 'God made the world.' But this is cheating. For it is using words which we, as adults, know have cash value only within the frontiers of abstract thought and religious symbolism. As a way of describing the 'why' of creation, the interpretation and value we set upon it and the sense of purpose with which we meet it, these words are inexhaustible in meaning, they are 'true'. But this capacity for abstract thinking is not developed in a child and he is incapable of understanding the statement 'God made the world' except as a crudely literal statement of historical fact. He inevitably misunderstands us, and we know he is bound to.

Why are we so afraid of distinguishing between fact and myth, between history and interpretation? The child deserves an honest answer to his question. He is interested in the 'how' of creation and we should give him a simple scientific or biological answer. He need not be deprived of the wonderful stories that have been told about creation so long as he is quite clear that we, while sharing his delight in them, understand them as stories. We too easily think of myth as a falsification of what is true, thus belittling it and degrading it and casting doubt upon the eternal truth enshrined within it. How ridiculous it would be if we insisted that the Sleeping Beauty was a real princess or that the Emperor really did walk in the procession with nothing on. It would not only rob them of their magic as stories but prevent us, as we grow older and wiser, from seeing that they are telling us something true about ourselves.

Our fear of distinguishing between fact and myth is even more serious when actual historical events are involved, such as the birth of Jesus. Here again we tend to use the two sorts of language indiscriminately, blindly disregarding the fact that the child, because he trusts us, will accept all we say as true, in the only sense in which he understands the word 'true', that is, literally. We tell him: 'Jesus was born in Bethlehem', and we tell him also: 'God sent his Son into the world'. The first of these statements is about what actually happened and the second is the interpretation we put upon it, the significance of the history in depth. To distinguish between the two is not to impoverish the story or belittle the event but precisely to preserve it in depth. To confuse the two is to risk reducing the event together with its interpretation to incredible fantasy.

When, however, we are dealing with historical events after the lapse of thousands of years, it is by no means easy to know at every point just where to draw the line between fact and myth. It is not even always easy to get to the bottom of what *actually* happened in an emotionally-charged incident the day before yesterday! And, again, we should not be afraid to say so, and we should be specially chary of forcing undue *historical* emphasis on precisely those points which are most questionable as history, as for example Mary's virginity. The important thing for us in sharing the event of Jesus' birth with our children is to represent faithfully the reality of experience it embodies. For the wonder and awe of the angels in the sky, the eager trustfulness of the shepherds, the total self-giving of Mary—these are real feelings and convictions. This was the way the early Christians who recorded the story felt about the man they had known and loved; this is the response drawn from us each Christmas as, remembering this birth, we commit ourselves to the daily incarnation of Love in our present-day world.

In focusing the story on the real feelings it records we are close to the child's own instinctive level of understanding, for it is real feelings that matter to him and it comes naturally to him to express these feelings through myth and symbol. A

APPENDIX II

symbol or myth is precious because of the intensity of the feeling it represents. When a small girl is playing at being mother she is giving expression to real feelings of motherliness. She knows she is 'only playing' and that she isn't really a mother, but we mustn't laugh at her or say: 'Of course you are only playing!', for if we belittle her show of 'being mother' we seem to her to be dismissing her feelings as unreal, which is an injustice. When she grows up she will be able to live out for herself in real life the relationships she has begun to apprehend and express through childhood play. The symbol of motherhood, the dolls of her childhood, will be set aside as naturally as once they were taken for granted.

If only we, the grown-ups, could respect our symbols in the same way! Some of them we need to use as long as we live because there is no other way of expressing or sharing the intensity of commitment and response they represent. Such a one is the symbol of God as Father. This is a 'true' symbol because it describes and defines the underlying reality of experience. How else can I express my response to this claim upon me which I certainly didn't invent but can't escape? Where else direct my promise of commitment? But too often we represent *our* symbols to the child as having value in themselves. We insist that God *is* a father and this sets up conflicts of guilt and unease in the child, because, if he is required to accept this as a literal fact, there comes a time when he must reject it as an adequate symbol of a deeper reality. He can't believe that God is *a* father, so he must find other ways of defining his commitment to life.

I recently heard a Christian minister rejoicing because he had overheard his three-year-old daughter talking to Jesus on her toy telephone and pouring out to him her pent-up feelings. I couldn't help wondering if he would have been equally pleased if she had confided in her teddy bear instead. I only hope that some years hence she will be allowed to discard her childhood fantasy without any guilty feelings that it is Christ she is betraying.

This brings me to the nub of the problem for the Christian

parent. In what light are we to present the man Jesus to our children? What role is he to play in their lives? As a sort of magic man, sent from another world, who might return at any moment? As a real historical figure about whom a lot of incredible legends have been woven? Or as a man of flesh and bone, a Jew of the first century A.D., who, in what he said and what he was, both defines and vindicates what we know to be most real about ourselves and our human situation, and who is at once both our hope and our surety? This depends on what we do know to be most real for ourselves, whether it corresponds to the reality we find in the New Testament, and whether in our own relationships we are able to share and communicate this reality with our children in a way which will help them to recognize its focus in Jesus Christ and in him to see through to its source.

Perhaps an illustration from real life will make my point. One of my children some time ago said she thought she knew why Peter's mother-in-law took to her bed. 'I expect she was so fed-up', she said, 'because Peter had been spending so much time wandering about Galilee with Jesus instead of looking after her daughter that she had a temperature and went to bed. And it was only when Jesus himself came to the house and she saw what sort of person he was that she wanted to get up and do things for people.' This, to some, might sound like a watering-down of a healing miracle, but to the child who described it in this way it is precisely the sort of wonderful transformation which can and does happen. Sometimes we are turned in on ourselves in resentment and self-pity until some gesture of love and caring turns us inside out and restores in us the capacity to give. This has happened to her, which is why the story rings true for her, and it is this sort of reality which she seems to understand the New Testament is about—this Love that has power to transform and heal, that creates purpose and meaning out of suffering, that holds in one Spirit the two or three gathered together.

The same point was made by the same child on another occasion. She had gone upstairs to fetch her Bible and discovered on the way that her sister was using her own painting pots. She came back and, flinging the Bible on the table, poured out her tale of wrath and recrimination. 'I'm going to make her give them all back to me.' I could only agree that, as they were hers, she was perfectly within her rights to demand them back and that perhaps she had better go and do so. She slid down off my knee saying, 'But you know I can't do that', and disappeared. I didn't see her again for an hour; but when she next appeared in the kitchen she was in a glow of happiness. They had shared out the paint pots and 'Do you know, Catherine lent me *her* brush and has been showing me how to paint!' Then she perched herself on the kitchen stool, looked at the Bible still lying on the table, and said: 'You know, Mummy, I have learnt more tonight than I would have done if we had done the Bible study.' And I had learnt more from her. For she had taught me that biblical truth is relevant to a child to the extent that it provides a definition or an explanation of what he already 'knows', in the deepest sense, from experience.

But biblical definition comes later, with a growing perception. Long before this, even when he is very small, we have a constant opportunity and responsibility to allow him to grow in the Spirit. Only in our love will the love of Christ be present to him, nor have we any hope later of explaining what, for example, atonement or reconciliation might mean unless he has already known for himself what it feels like to forgive and be forgiven, and to be accepted even at one's worst. This is the language of the living Word in which we communicate to our children what we know is true for us and hope will be true for them. This is living itself, in its fullest sense, with no religious or pious overtones, no forcing of a premature definition but a quiet nuturing of the soil in the hope of future growth.

If we take seriously this underlying responsibility of spiritual education in and through our relationship with our children, we can be free to be much less anxious than we often are as Christian parents about the religious instruction we give them. We are far too anxious to moralize about and interpret the stories of the Bible, especially for example the parables, not only ruining them as stories but killing their capacity to speak directly to the children. This was brought home to me in a recent television broadcast on Sunday Schools in which I was involved. The programme began with a film of what was reckoned to be a good Sunday School. The children had been learning, or rather the teacher had been instructing them in, the story of the healing of the paralytic. The interviewer then questioned the children about their lesson. When asked what they enjoyed most about Sunday School, several said that they 'liked the stories'. When they were asked what this particular story had been about, they managed well to begin with but got very confused at the point where the teacher had apparently tried to force an interpretation and had clearly lost their attention. They tried, some more successfully than others, to reproduce 'correct' answers, but the magic of the story had gone. This is surely not the way to make the Word live for our children. We should rather so present it, telling the stories in the first instance in our own words, as to kindle their imagination and provoke their interest. The most haunting stories for us as children are the ones that ultimately elude us and leave us wondering. These we return to in later life hoping they will at last reveal their secret. And they often do.

Prayer in Childhood

No discussion of the Christian education of children would be complete without asking ourselves searching questions about what prayer means in childhood. Here I do not attempt to do more than describe one family situation; it is, if you like, the one piece of case history about which I have any detailed or inside knowledge. But I believe it may reflect many similar situations, and perhaps bring to the surface some of the conflicts and uncertainties which we, as parents or teachers, can hardly yet dare to admit. The subject raises for me many questions which I find very uncomfortable, some even painful, but I cannot pretend I don't hear the questions! However we

APPENDIX II

define God it must be in terms of the truth, and ultimately truth will out, and, in the Spirit, we have no need to fear it.

When they are small, children in a Christian home enjoy saying prayers. In the first place, it is something mother does with you and that in itself makes it enjoyable. It brings her comfortably close and you have not only all her attention but her smiling approval as you gradually learn to join in. Saying prayers becomes part of the accepted pattern of life and this is important. Pattern helps you to get your bearings and to know what to expect; it makes you feel safe. This is why you sometimes need to prod her if she deviates from a phrase which, for you, has become part of the pattern: 'You forgot to say. . . .' Perhaps, too, this is the function that Assembly plays for the small child when he finds himself in the larger community of the Infants' School—a focus where this larger family expresses its togetherness, its belonging, its purpose, and where he can feel his own place within it.

My first question then is this: Is 'saying prayers' for the small child one means of securing his relationships? Is what really matters to him having someone who will listen to him and take him seriously as a person, someone with whom he can feel safe enough to talk his thoughts? And where does God fit into this activity from the child's point of view? Perhaps 'God' as a definition of this depth of relationship, this shared openness, is only necessary to the grown-ups?

My next question is prompted by the 'cooling-off' phase, coinciding with the time when the child is being weaned from saying prayers with mother. What evidence have we that, apart from moral or emotional pressure (that is, in order to be good or to please the grown-ups), any child beyond the infant stage *wants* to say prayers if left to himself? One of my informants tells me: 'I can remember Daddy coming in to tuck me up and asking me if I had said my prayers and would I like him to say them with me. I always liked it when he did but I wouldn't have thought about it otherwise.'

J., who is nine, says no prayers by herself as far as I know. She joins in passively when we say prayers together as a family, always taking care to sidle up to mother as close as she can before we begin. She can't articulate any thoughts about prayer: a shy 'I don't know *what* it means' was all she said when I asked what she thought and was clearly relieved when I left it at that and didn't go on about it. Yet in church she seriously and audibly joins in the recited prayers and is most meticulous about following the service in her Prayer Book. This again I would say is a question of security, of being able to follow the customs of the community so that you really feel you belong, like learning the ways of a new school.

But this gives little indication of what I sense to be the real spiritual activity going on inside her and in practice bears little relation to it. She was, for example, at an early age suddenly faced with the reality of separation and the fear that the person who mattered most to her might die. Whether this fear is allowed to fester into mistrust and resentment or can be acknowledged and lived with, is not a matter of chance, but it cannot be worked out at the level of 'saying prayers'. It is a question of being open to any opportunity of facing it that may occur not only in words but through a shared and reassuring relationship. When your real fear is 'When Mummy goes out of the room, it's as if she goes away from me for ever', you are not likely to be comforted at that moment by talk of God or Jesus. It is Mummy you want, not God, and if he is offered as a comforting substitute you will only resent him, and he may even for this reason subsequently be found inadequate as a definition of a love stronger than death which will never let you down.

This distinction between the activity of prayer, which I would define as a trusting openness or a readiness to communicate, and 'saying prayers' is borne out by the rather devastating encounter I had with B. aged twelve. She was more articulate, but she spared no punches. 'Prayer', she said—'well, it is sort of thinking, when you don't know what to do and you think about it and it sort of comes to you.' And later: 'God isn't really a person but it helps to imagine he is and you can talk to him.' 'It is as if he is your mind.' I asked how this was different from just thinking. She said it wasn't really, and if she 'lived in darkest Africa' and hadn't heard of God she would do it just the same way 'only I wouldn't know I was talking to God'. I asked her if praying was always to do with having to decide what to do—did she ever pray when she was feeling very glad or happy about something? The answer was instantaneous: 'Oh no; you're too glad and happy to think about it'. Do we, in fact, tend to think of thanksgiving more on the level of the thank-you letter than the spontaneous joy of receiving? Then I asked her why it helped more to talk to God than to some other person. 'Well, it's best of all if I can talk to you, of course, but you aren't always there. Anyhow, sometimes it's something you can't talk to anyone else about because it would sound silly.' Where, I thought, does this get us? Does it mean that praying to God by yourself is a substitue for human relationships when they fail you or you daren't commit yourself to them?

On the subject of saying prayers, either as a family or in church, she was uncompromising. 'Other people's words are no use. When you are praying', she said scathingly, 'you are thinking. You don't have to think it all in words.' She insisted that she didn't understand a word of what went on in church and added: 'I don't even understand the Lord's Prayer.' But how can you at twelve, if you don't think of God as a person in a place called heaven? At this point, I suggested rather desperately that perhaps if I tried to *explain* the words a bit more . . . ? 'Well, of course, it might help, but it would be so boring!'

I retired from this encounter feeling very shaken. Perhaps it was true then after all that I was depriving my children of a heritage. This had been said to me recently by someone I loved and respected who felt they were not, for example, learning to worship and adore in the traditional language of the psalms and collects. Have I then left them only with a prayer-shaped blank and no language to fill it out? I seem myself in recent years to have kicked away so many of the ladders by which I have thankfully climbed, but have I in doing so left the children no route to follow? At least I had been given no pat answers, I thought wryly, nothing that sounded remotely like a correct Catechism response; and perhaps this might be counted on the credit side in a bishop's household!

I remembered my short-lived attempt, springing from a guilty sense of neglected duty, to evoke just this sort of response. We had proceeded for some time very politely and attentively with the clauses of the Catechism and I thought I was doing rather well, until one day I happened to overhear their own version:

> What is your name?
> Elephant's child.
> Who gave you this name?
> My tall aunt the ostrich, my broad aunt the hippopotamus and my hairy uncle the baboon.
> What did they for you?
> They did spank me for my satiable curtiosity.

Once again I retired much chastened. I should have known they would see through me. Nevertheless, this problem of their rightful heritage bothered me and I was beginning to feel the millstone dragging about my neck.

Grace and benediction came, as often, unexpectedly but most aptly. C. who is now 15 had just come in from school and was telling me about the SCM discussion they had just had about why God allows earthquakes. ('No one seemed to remember that we had had a geography lesson on the causes of earthquakes earlier this morning!') Somehow we got on to the subject of prayer, and she began to describe to me what it means to her. She is still young enough to remember something of how this conscious understanding came to her and old enough to begin to express it. I will try to report her faithfully.

Prayer, she says, is keeping your mind open so that God's thoughts can come into it. God is a sort of power which is there for us. She has never been able to think of him as a person on the other end of a wire whom she can talk to. She remembers being taken aback when they had a scripture lesson

APPENDIX II

about prayer at school. They were told there were five different aspects to it . . . that this is what prayer is . . . and this is how you set about it. . . . 'You don't think to question them when they tell you things at school and I thought I must have just missed out on something and I'd better try a bit harder.' So she says she tried doing it the way they said, but it didn't mean anything to her. She was determined to do it properly in the right words, 'with all the "thees" and "thous".' But her mind kept drifting off and she would have to start all over again, 'like having to unpick a piece of needlework that has gone wrong'. In the end she gave it up as it was just getting her nowhere. 'I wanted to do something, but I knew it wasn't this.' She decided that this was real for some people because they had always been used to it, 'like cleaning their teeth', but it just wasn't real for her.

The millstone began to drag again and I asked her if she thought it would have been easier for her if she had always been expected to kneel down by her bed and say her prayers as naturally as cleaning her teeth. 'Oh no', she said, 'because then I should have just felt terribly guilty about not doing it.' As it is, she can accept quite naturally, with none of the uneasiness I would myself still feel, that when her friends come to stay they each have different ways of praying. One kneels down for five minutes before getting into bed, the other gets straight into bed with her Bible-reading and waits for what comes. 'Sometimes it comes from what I have just been reading, sometimes it's something I've read in the paper that day, sometimes I'm praying for somebody. And I can go on as long as I need to.' Here I asked her the same question I had put to B: 'How is this different from just thinking? After all, we all lie in bed thinking.' 'Oh, but it's quite different. Thinking is anything that comes into your head—Mrs Bloggins out in her backyard hanging up her washing, or anything—and what point is there in that unless of course there is something you can do for Mrs Bloggins? With praying, there is a purpose to it. There is generally something you can do about it.' 'Sometimes I find I'm thinking in this way as I'm cycling up the hill to school. But you can't stop and put it all into the proper sort of prayer language.'

But I was still worried about this 'prayer language', this heritage that had been entrusted to me to pass on. Did it in fact mean nothing? C. said that when she was younger the words we use in church were absolutely meaningless to her. 'I didn't even try to listen until we got to the Gospel' (which we had generally prepared together as a family the night before). She hardly ever understood what the sermon was about and just sat and thought about other things. But recently, she says, words have begun to 'come alive'. Sometimes, for example, she will recognize in the collect a definition of what she herself feels and wants to express. 'It is as if I have now got something to fill out the words with.' This was the clue I had been looking for and I should like to return to it, because it has helped me to understand how we can perhaps pass on this heritage of prayer in a way which is real both for us and for the children.

But first of all I want to mention another thing we talked out because it offered a parallel clue. I asked C. what it meant to her to pray for other people. A little while ago, she said, we were praying in church for Mrs Kennedy and she wondered what good this could do. 'But', she thought to herself, 'it is minding about her that matters. It is as if your caring adds to the general store of caring in the world, and it may be needed anywhere. It must help to know that people care about you, and it helped me too to pray for her because it made me more caring as a person.' I asked her how she thought she had come to learn to think about it in this way and she said: 'You just have to work it out for yourself.'

And I thought to myself how true it was for her, though she has no conscious memory of her early encounter with this process. I remembered the occasion almost fifteen years ago when she had been returned to me from hospital with a fairly common but, in her case, acute digestive malformation which it was too dangerous to put right by surgery. 'She may adjust to it', I was told. They could do no more for her. Like thousands of mothers before me, I swore grimly that I *would* keep my baby alive, and for a month we struggled until both she and I were exhausted in the process. And then one day surrounded and supported by the prayerful caring of friends and neighbours, we took her into the little chapel near our home to lay our hands upon her, and I came out knowing that a burden had been lifted from me. C. is right. What she calls the 'general store of caring' may be needed anywhere, and it is when we have none of our own resources left that we depend upon each other for healing. 'You have to work it out for yourself', as she says, but the process begins further back than we can consciously remember.

Our Children and the Christian Inheritance

Perhaps I may, by way of conclusion, draw together some of these strands and suggest how we may, as parents and teachers, make it possible for our children to step into their inheritance.

First of all, we must distinguish between the attitude and mind of prayer and 'saying prayers'. The first I would describe as trusting and exposing oneself, with no holds barred, to what is most real within oneself and the world about one, and responding to it. This for the child is an unconscious activity and is learnt during childhood in and through his personal relationships. A child can only learn to trust by trusting other people and it is those closest to him, his parents and his teachers, with whom he needs to be able to communicate his trust. If he can expose himself safely in his encounters with them, if they can tune in to his unexpressed needs and share with him his joy and his sense of wonder and mystery, he is all the time being helped to build up a prayerful response to life. He is beginning to work it out for himself on his pulses, he is acquiring that content of experience with which later he will be able to 'fill out the words'.

Nothing, I believe, is a substitute for this depth of shared personal relationship, no amount of saying prayers will do instead. Indeed, I am inclined to think that the urge to define, to wrap up our response to life in tidy parcels of words, is essentially an adult activity which develops gradually with the capacity for abstract thought and our need to express and communicate what we believe. We do not need to overburden the child with reasoned explanations of what the Lord's Prayer means but to enrich his life with the reality of its content. It is enough that the words should be available and familiar, ready for the time when he is consciously aware of the reality and wants to express it. Perhaps we worry about whether the words have meaning for him because we shrink from involving ourselves too closely in the reality they convey. Daily bread and forgiveness, encouragement and protection, a sense of reverence and a hint of glory; these are his basic human needs and he looks to us for them.

What then of 'saying prayers', of the verbal framework of praying? I would say that this is helpful so long as it isn't too demanding. A familiar pattern, whether in family prayers, school Assembly or church, enables a child to express himself as a member of the community and to share its commitment. But he ought to be allowed to sit lightly to it, to accept it naturally without overtones of moral obligation. If there is too much of it or it is too oppressive, it overwhelms and confuses him; if it seems to expect some sort of individual, as opposed to corporate, response from him, it makes him feel uncomfortable and inadequate. But, always, the praying together must express and define a reality of mutual caring and shared relationship, and never be allowed to become a substitute for it. We can't pretend we have resolved some hidden tension by mentioning it at prayer time, though this may be the first step towards it. Unless we are prepared to follow it through at the deeper and less comfortable level of person to person encounter, the praying itself becomes a sort of escape.

What form 'saying prayers' will take will vary in each school or home; each needs, as it were, to evolve its own simple 'liturgy' according to what seems to fit most naturally into the life of the group. Here I would make two simple practical observations. The first is that, in any living community, the 'liturgy', the form of worship, is not likely to be fixed and unchanging. It is not just a question, even, of having an outward form which is flexible and resilient enough to be adapted and varied. One sometimes finds one needs to change the form itself, or even to rest it entirely, if sheer usage and familiarity induces boredom or the physical circumstances change, though this is perhaps more apparent in the constantly changing conditions of home life, than in school or church.

The second point is that our time and space scales are so contracted in this mechanized age, the world is so much smaller and time goes so much faster, that our smallest units, like our coins, are hardly usable. In many spheres of activity it is getting less and less possible to operate with each day as a unit of time, and certainly in our situation weekly family prayer and Bible-reading (centring round what the children call our 'family supper', when we break and share bread together) is, at the moment, what seems right for us. We can look forward to it and value it without being oppressed by the speed at which it comes round.

In all this discussion, however, there is nothing that defines this attitude of prayerful response in specifically Christian terms without the dimension provided in the Bible by the history of God's claim upon man and man's response to it. Without this, both as springboard and life-line, I could not have plunged into the discussion at all. But perhaps it is no accident that I have been able to get so far with it without referring to the Bible except indirectly, as it may perhaps indicate how we and our children may be brought to the point of rediscovering in the Bible the supreme definition and interpretation of our human experience and situation. For here, in a flash of recognition, we see ourselves and the relationship in which we are held. Just as for C. the words of the Church's prayers begin to 'come alive', so we come to discover that we have a content of experience to 'fill out' the history and stories of the Bible. We recognize the Old Testament description of the indwelling of God, for we have begun to know it; the call to Samuel comes also to us, we struggle with Jacob's adversary, and suffer with Job. We have begun to share the response of Jesus to his Father and to feel the life of the Spirit stirring within us. If this can be the context in which our children can gradually learn to identify the familiar stories with what is real for them, this heritage also will not be lost to them.

It is the particular problem of our generation of parents and teachers to know how to share with our children the depth and dimension of Christian experience in terms which do not distort it. But they themselves provide the clues if we will listen. As children they need help in 'working it out for themselves', below the conscious level, in their relationships with those they trust, so that later on they have the content of experience with which they may 'fill out the words' and the tradition they have inherited.

INDEX

Acland, R., 69
Allan, T., 91
Athanasius, 61
Augustine, 61

Bakunin, M., 104
Barth, K., 34f., 61
Basil, 61
Baum, G., 45
Baxter, K. M., 75
Bea, A., 9
Beeson, T., 91
Berger, P., 52, 63
Berton, P., 6
Bettenson, H., 11
Birch, L. C., 33
Blamires, H., 51
Blank, J. de, 91
Bliss, K., 55
Bodelschwinck, G. von, 32
Bonhoeffer, D., 18, 23, 26, 33, 98, 107, 110, 121f.
Borelli, Fr, 104
Boulard, F., 71
Briggs, G. W., 84
Brunner, E., 34
Buber, M., 116
Buddha, 41
Buren, P. van, 19, 24, 108
Byers, C. M., 27

Calvin, J., 61
Camus, A., 112f.
Carter, S., 114
Casalis, G., 91

Chadwick, W. O., 16, 19, 21
Chardin, T. de, 33
Congar, Y., 54
Cope, G., 70
Cox, H. G., 52, 92, 94f.

Davies, D. R., 15
Davies, J. G., 85
Davis, C., 60-2, 73f.
Dix, G., 85f.
Dostoievski, F., 113

Edwards, D. L., 10, 21
Emmerich, R. S., 98
Engels, F., 112

Feuerbach, L., 112
Fisher, G. F., 20
Flew, A. G. N., 108, 119
Forsyth, P. T., 61
Freud, S., 112
Furlong, M., 28

Gaitskell, H., 76
Gibbs, M., 54, 69
Goldman, R., 69

Hamilton, W., 14, 23, 36, 115
Heinzelmann, G., 60
Heuvel, A. van den, 14, 27, 81, 87, 99
Hindley, J. C., 13
Hippolytus, 85
Hocking, M., 91
Hoekendijk, J. C., 72, 85, 89

Hooker, R., 61
Huss, J., 16
Huxley, J., 108f., 119

James, E., 83, 96
Jarrett-Kerr, M., 75

Keble, J., 84
Kenrick, B., 85
King, M. L., 104
Koestler, A., 14
Kraemer, H., 54

Laplace, P. S., 107, 109
Lloyd, R., 10, 22
Loukes, H., 69
Luther, M., 11, 18f., 32f., 35, 61

McBrien, R. P., 49
McGill, A. C., 75
Macmurray, J., 116
Mahommed, 41
Maritain, J., 112
Marx, K., 112
Maurice, F. D., 12
Michonneau, G., 112
Morton, T. R., 18, 54, 69, 89
Munden, C. E., 31

Napoleon, 107
Niebuhr, H. Richard, 62, 71
Niebuhr, Reinhold, 34f., 72
Niemöller, M., 32
Nietzsche, F. W., 112
Novak, M., 29, 95

O'Connor, E., 85

Parrinder, G., 12
Paul, L., 55, 61, 96

Pelz, W. and L., 18, 109
Pierre, Abbé, 104
Pike, J., 39
Proops, M., 113
Proudhon, J., 112

Quoist, M., 85

Raines, R. A., 91
Root, H., 73, 76

Sartre, J.-P., 112
Smith, R. A., 11
Southcott, E. W., 91
Stacey, N., 102
Symanowski, H., 32, 85

Temple, W., 20
Tillich, P., 12, 30, 33, 44f., 47, 115f., 120
Torrance, T. F., 10

Vahanian, G., 14
Vidler, A. R., 11f., 15, 18, 23, 28
Vries, P. de, 113

Wain, J., 73
Webber, G. W., 85
Weber, H. R., 55
Wedel, T. O., 32
Wesley, J., 61
Wickham, E. R., 16, 68f.
Williams, C. W., 31, 75, 88f., 91-3, 103-5
Wilson, H., 76
Winter, G., 64-6
Wren-Lewis, J., 57
Wycliffe, J., 16